Easter Island,
with its inhospitable coasts
and its meager vegetation, provides a stark
contrast to the green paradise of Polynesia.
The colossal works of an impoverished people
have engendered a very different myth
from that of the noble savage. In fact,
some people have refused to believe that
the statues are the result of
mere human capabilities.

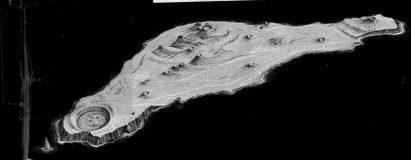

After several months of labor, stone giants were finally born from the eroded flanks of Rano Raraku volcano.

The legendary statues, each detached from its
rocky keel, were
dragged down the
slope and then set up in

The statues were transported, sometimes for
more than twelve miles, and then hoisted onto

CONTENTS

EASTER ISLAND
MYSTERY OF THE STONE GIANTS

Catherine and Michel Orliac

DISCOVERIES

HARRY N. ABRAMS, INC., PUBLISHERS

"In the middle of the Great Ocean, in a region where no one ever passes, there is a mysterious and isolated island; there is no land in the vicinity and, for more than eight hundred leagues in all directions, empty and moving vastness surrounds it. It is planted with tall, monstrous statues, the work of some now-vanished race, and its past remains an enigma."

Pierre Loti, *L'Ile de Pâques*, 1872

CHAPTER I
EUROPEANS DISCOVER EASTER ISLAND

Before Easter Island fell prey to fantasy and imagination, it aroused the curiosity of explorers in the South Pacific during the 18th and 19th centuries.

Left: Statues at *ahu* Nau Nau, Anakena.

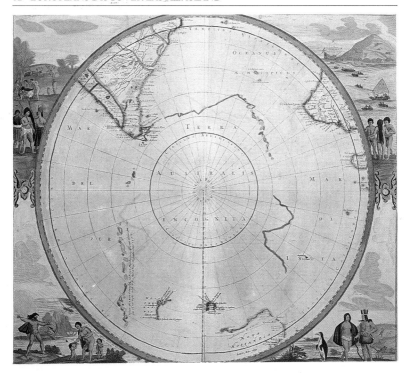

In 1721 Jacob Roggeveen Sailed Through the Southern Hemisphere in Search of an Island Glimpsed by the Buccaneer Edward Davis

During the first crossing of the Pacific by a European seafarer, in 1521, Ferdinand Magellan passed between the Tuamotu and the Marquesas archipelagos without seeing one island. Two centuries were to pass before the discovery of Easter Island. Inadequate navigational instruments, fragile ships, and lack of method in the organization of expeditions were all weaknesses in the face of the vast Pacific, and the geography of the Great Ocean would long remain a mystery. Until the 18th century Polynesia was known only from brief and violent contacts between the Portuguese and the islanders of the Marquesas and the Tuamotus.

Most 17th-century geographers believed in the existence of a continent in the South Pacific. The icebergs that Jacob Roggeveen saw toward latitude 62° S could, he believed, come only from the breakup of great rivers in an unknown continent that extended to the South Pole.

Opposite: A woman from Easter Island.

On 21 August 1721 Dutch commander Jacob Roggeveen left the Netherlands at the head of a fleet of three ships equipped by the West India Company, which held a monopoly on trade with the Americas. Roggeveen was setting out in search of a land that the English buccaneer Edward Davis had spotted in the South Pacific in 1687. Davis' discovery gave 18th-century geographers evidence for the old theory that there existed in the South Pacific a supposed southern continent, a *Terra Australis Incognita,* that ensured the equilibrium of the globe by counterbalancing the weight of the lands in the northern hemisphere. The search for this continent, which seemed to slip away as the Pacific revealed its mysteries, was to draw navigators to the South Seas for years to come.

On the Evening of Easter Sunday, 5 April 1722, the Dutch Sailors Spotted an Unknown Land

After approaching the island, Roggeveen noticed that the line of the coast did not correspond to Davis' descriptions. He named this tiny island "Paasch Eyland" (Easter Island). The first contact with the inhabitants took place the next morning: An islander climbed on board quite casually, taking a particular interest in the ship and its rigging. With great curiosity the crew observed this man who began to dance when the ship's band struck up a tune. After this jolly companion departed, the ship was soon invaded by a noisy group of visitors who "were so bold that they

"The inhabitants of this island do not seem to exceed six or seven hundred souls, and above two-thirds of those we saw were males. They either have but few females among them, or else many were restrained from making their appearance, during our stay."

James Cook,
A Voyage Towards the South Pole, and Round the World.... In the Years 1772–1775,
Vol. I, 1777

took the hats and caps of the sailors from their heads and jumped with their plunder overboard"; in the captain's cabin the tablecloth disappeared through the window. That afternoon a detachment of sailors was sent ashore with peaceful intentions. The islanders had varied reactions: Some made friendly gestures, but others threw stones. Shots rang out in the middle of a general tumult, and as many as a dozen islanders were killed. The crowd dispersed, then returned to the shore with presents and standards as a sign of peace, but after this slaughter the Dutch went back to their vessels.

Roggeveen resumed his voyage on 10 April in search of the southern continent. His brief visit had enabled him to see gigantic statues, which he believed were formed from clay. His account, together with that of his companion Carl Friederich Behrens, revealed to the West the existence of a strange island populated with colossal statues. Then, for almost half a century, the island was forgotten by European navigators, until Spain, worried by the inroads made by the French and English into the Pacific, sent out expeditions to reconnoiter the lands close to its South American colonies.

Fifty Years Later the Easter Islanders Saw Sails on the Horizon Once Again

In December 1770 two Spanish ships commanded by Felipe

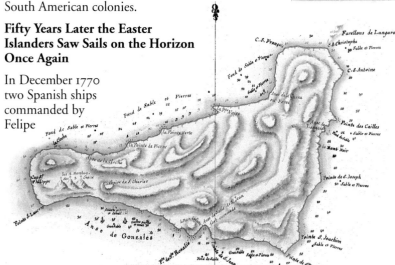

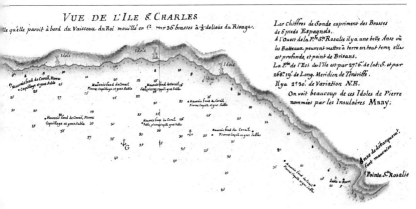

Ainsi paroissent les Montagnes de l'Ile du Mouillage G.

González y Haedo, who was also in search of Davis' land, arrived within sight of Easter Island. Despite a few thefts by the islanders, relations remained cordial. On 15 December 1770, the Spanish took possession of the island in the name of His Majesty Carlos III, king of Spain. In his honor, it was baptized Isla de San Carlos. The island's chiefs were invited to place their mark at the bottom of the official document; three of them drew signs similar to those that would be read later on the wooden *kohau rongo rongo* tablets. González y Haedo drew up the first map of the island before setting sail again. His stay had lasted six days.

In December 1770 the Spanish anchored in Hanga o Honu Bay, which they christened "González Cove." On the map they drew up, they carefully marked the three crosses they had set up on the hills of Poike (opposite, far left) when they took possession of the island.

On 14 March 1774 the Famous Captain Cook Called at Easter Island

After his fruitful 1769 expedition in the South Seas, the English navigator had only one desire, "to go beyond former discoverers; and to continue to Britain the reputation of taking the lead of all nations, in exploring the globe." In a final search for the southern continent, Captain Cook crossed the South Pacific as far as the ice floes. After this dangerous and futile exploration, he reached Easter Island. He anchored his ships, the *Resolution* and the *Adventure*, in Hanga Roa Bay in the hope of finding drinking water and fresh provisions for the sick, who had developed scurvy. The islanders received them as they had received their predecessors—with friendliness and pilfering.

Given the scarcity of provisions and drinkable water, the English expedition stayed at Hanga Roa for only three days, yet the descriptions by Cook and his companions were to bring the island the fame it has since enjoyed.

Portrait of James Cook by the 18th-century artist John Webber.

Cook did not encourage navigators to stop at Easter Island: "No nation need contend for the honour of the discovery of this island; as there can be few places which afford less convenience for shipping than it does. Here is no safe anchorage; no wood for fuel; nor any fresh water worth taking on board. Nature has been exceedingly sparing of her favours to this spot. As every thing must be raised by dint of labour, it cannot be supposed the inhabitants plant much more than is sufficient for themselves; and as they are but few in number, they cannot have much to spare to supply the wants of visitant strangers."

One of these two statues (opposite below) on the side of Rano Raraku bears an engraving of a European ship from the fleet of Roggeveen, González, or Cook.

On the Evening of 9 April 1786 the First French Expedition Reached the Island

Monuments from Easter Island, as drawn by Duché de Vancy, the artist on the La Pérouse expedition.

King Louis XVI asked Jean-François de Galaup, Comte de La Pérouse, to undertake a great expedition in the South Seas to "discover lands that escaped the eye of Cook." The *Astrolabe* and the *Boussole*, commanded by La Pérouse, anchored on 9 April in Hanga Roa Bay, also known as Cook's Bay. The following morning, at 8 o'clock, La Pérouse set foot on the island, accompanied by a few officers and seventy crew members. Like the English captain, he was astonished by the inhabitants' behavior, as they stole everything they could lay their hands on: "The women offered their favors to all those who would make them a present... and while our attention was attracted by the women, we were robbed of our hats and handkerchiefs." In order to avoid any trouble, La Pérouse had to announce to his crew that

he would replace any stolen hats and handkerchiefs. Two expeditions were formed to explore the island. The first, commanded by La Pérouse himself, visited the monuments, platforms, houses, and plantations around Cook's Bay. The second was led by Viscount Paul Antoine de Langle, accompanied by several officers and the gardener from "the king of France's gardens." They were to penetrate the island's interior, "sow seeds…examine the soil, plants, cultivation, population, monuments, and generally everything that may be of interest about this extraordinary

"As for the women, I dare not decide whether they are common to a whole district, and the children to the republic: Certain it is that no Indian appeared to have the authority of a husband over any one of the women, and if they are private property, it is a kind of which the possessors are very liberal."

Jean-François de Galaup, Comte de La Pérouse, *A Voyage Round the World in the Years 1785–1788*, Vol. II, 1798

people." While they were exploring, the gardener sowed cabbages, carrots, beets, maize, and pumpkins, as well as seeds of orange and lemon trees and cotton plants, while goats, sheep, and pigs were given to the inhabitants. Bernizet, the expedition's geographer, drew up an accurate plan of the monumental sanctuaries and the large dwellings.

At the end of this excursion, the sailors and officers went back on board, and the two ships continued their exploration of the Pacific. La Pérouse's fleet disappeared mysteriously in 1788. Thirty years passed before traces of the shipwreck were found in the Santa Cruz Islands, east of the Solomon Islands.

1805: The First Abductions of Easter Islanders

La Pérouse was the last of the humanist seafarers from the Age of Enlightenment to visit the island, albeit briefly; Easter Island's history then entered an era of darkness and death. Starting at the beginning of the 19th century, adventurers and whalers inflicted numerous cruelties on the islanders. First, in 1805, the crew of the American schooner *Nancy* captured

This early-19th-century Italian engraving (below), after an original drawing from La Pérouse's voyage, represents the illustrious navigator at the foot of one of the numerous statues in Cook's Bay. Seated, Bernizet, the expedition's geographer, draws the monument's plan. Opposite: Two engravings based on the voyage.

twelve men and ten women after a bloody struggle, intending to use these unfortunates as slaves for seal hunting on the Juan Fernández Islands. After three days' sailing, the prisoners were allowed on the *Nancy*'s bridge. The men threw themselves into the sea and swam desperately in the direction of their island; despite several attempts to save them, they all drowned. This disaster did not stop the captain of the *Nancy* from organizing more raids on the island to recruit men by force. Following these repeated crimes the Easter Islanders' attitude toward foreigners became frankly hostile.

The Terrorized Islanders Greeted Seafarers with Volleys of Stones

In 1816 the Russian scientific expedition led by Otto von Kotzebue, commander of the *Rurik*, tried to disembark on the beach of Hanga Roa. The Russians were received with a hail of stones. On a second attempt, under the cover of musket fire, they reached the land; they found themselves in the midst of a crowd of aggressive men with painted faces who "danced with the most grotesque contortions." The islanders grew increasingly threatening and forced the sailors to retreat and respond with gunshots.

Nearly ten years later, in 1825, the *Blossom*, commanded by Frederick William Beechey, anchored in Cook's Bay. "It is not easy," Beechey wrote, "to imagine the picture that was presented by this motley

Dance of the Easter Islanders on board *La Vénus* during the visit of the French admiral Abel Dupetit-Thouars in 1838 (above). Below: Russian commander Otto von Kotzebue attempts to land in 1816.

crowd…all hallooing to the extent of their lungs, and pressing upon the boats with all sorts of grimaces and gestures." The tumult was at its height when the seamen reached the shore. In the confusion, volleys of stones seriously wounded several sailors, who shot at the crowd, killing several men, including a chief. Beechey's men left the island that same day.

No doubt the islanders had not forgotten the visit three years earlier of the whaling vessel *Pindos*, whose crew had carried off young girls to "amuse" the sailors; soon thrown overboard, they had to swim back to the beach. The second-in-command of the whaler, a man named Walden, had taken aim at an islander and killed him—for fun!

The Peruvian Slave-Hunters Decimated the Island's Population

The year of 1862 was a decisive one in the history of Easter Island's people, since they almost did not

Immense colonies of seabirds live on the islands off the coasts of Peru, Colombia, and Chile; for centuries their droppings have formed thick layers of guano, a powerful fertilizer, rich in nitrogen. Guano was exploited intensively during the 19th century. Left: Collecting guano.

survive the horrible exactions of the slave traders. That year, Peruvian ships were in search of prey in the archipelagos of Polynesia. These slave ships had a common objective: to carry off men and women and sell them as slaves to the companies mining guano on the Peruvian coast. In this prosperous business, the work proved to be particularly arduous, and the workforce was lacking.

On the morning of 12 December, ninety sailors disembarked and laid out some cheap goods on the beach to attract the Easter Islanders. When a large number of islanders were assembled, most of them busy examining the goods, the slave traders attacked and captured them. Some escaped by climbing up the cliff, or by throwing themselves into the sea; many were massacred. Those who had gone to the vessels were clapped in irons down in the hold. Among the prisoners were King Kaimakoi and his son Maurata as well as the priests and learned men of the island (called *maori*), keepers of the ancestral culture.

A Thousand Easter Islanders, No Doubt Half the Island's Population, Were Captured

After several months of forced labor in the guano mines, nine hundred of the Easter Islanders perished from disease and ill treatment. The

Laborers resting (below) and unloading guano wagons (above).

bishop of Tahiti, Mgr. Tepano Jaussen, used his influence with the government in Lima to obtain the repatriation of the surviving prisoners. During the return voyage, eighty-five of the one hundred repatriated islanders died of smallpox and tuberculosis; the fifteen

wretched survivors disembarked on Easter Island and rapidly contaminated the rest of the population. The island was then transformed into a mass grave. By the end of this murderous epidemic, to which were added the effects of internal wars, only six hundred inhabitants remained.

The Arrival of the Missionaries

Eugène Eyraud, the first European to settle on the island, was a member of the religious community of the brothers of the Sacré-Coeur of Picpus. A former mechanic, he joined the fathers of the Holy Spirit as a novice and left Chile for Tahiti with other missionaries in 1862. He arrived in Hanga Roa on 2 January 1864. Harassed and robbed by the islanders, Eyraud stayed on the island for nine months. On 11 October 1864 he went back to Chile, destitute.

However, seventeen months later, on 27 March 1866, he returned and settled on Easter Island for good, accompanied by Father Hippolyte Roussel and three Polynesians from Mangareva Island. At first the islanders were opposed to the missionaries. However, once they became accustomed to their presence, they were "won over by the word of God"; in less than ten months Eyraud and his friends acquired tremendous influence over the population.

In October 1866, Father Gaspard Zumbohm and Brother Théodule Escolan joined the two missionaries, bringing with them saplings of fruit trees, seeds, and a few animals, including a cow. The island's population was then concentrated at Hanga Roa and Vaihu, where the missionaries dispensed their teaching. Christianity made rapid progress: The

Above: Brother Eyraud's tomb, close to the church of Hanga Roa.

"I intend to go to Easter Island. Would you therefore be so kind as to grant those Easter Islanders who are living on Tahiti and who ask to return home permission to board the ship with me.... I shall willingly take care of the cost of their passage."
Letter from Brother Eyraud to the Very Reverend Father Superior General, 12 November 1863

first converts were the children, then the young people, and finally the women; the old chiefs remained the most resistant. "The chances of triumph look more certain from day to day, and the hour of Providence seems to have arrived for the inhabitants of Easter Island. The mission became established at the moment when the work of destruction was nearing its final limits: Destruction of the material order, destruction of the moral order," wrote Brother Eyraud on 22 December 1866. By the time of his death in 1868 all the islanders had been converted.

The Removal of the "Stolen Friend"

It was not enough to have almost totally annihilated a population and destroyed its culture; it was also necessary to pillage the riches of its past. The

The "Stolen Friend," being transported on the *Topaze* (above), is now in the Museum of Mankind in London.

Western nations busied themselves with this task. In the year of Brother Eyraud's death, an American navy warship, the *Topaze*, called at Easter Island. After visiting the main sites, the ship's sailors, helped by three hundred islanders, destroyed a house in the ceremonial village of Orongo to extract the great stone statue that came to be known as *Hoa haka nana ia* (the "Stolen Friend").

A French Adventurer Put the Island to the Sword

The laborious undertaking of the missionaries was

jeopardized by the arrival in April 1868 of a French adventurer, Jean-Baptiste Dutrou-Bornier. This former captain in the merchant navy eventually settled on Easter Island to raise livestock. In 1869 he "bought," for a few pieces of cloth, the most fertile lands on the island at Mataveri, with the aim of starting an agricultural operation. This violent, greedy, and unscrupulous man soon clashed with the missionaries; serious incidents broke out in 1870 between the islanders from the Hanga Roa Catholic mission and those from Mataveri who had joined Dutrou-Bornier. Dutrou-Bornier's men finally destroyed Hanga Roa and Vaihu. The situation became intolerable, and Mgr. Jaussen ordered the missionaries to leave the island.

The same year, John Brander, an associate of Dutrou-Bornier, sent a ship to Easter Island to recruit men for his plantations in Tahiti; three hundred islanders preferred exile to remaining under the tyrant's domination. The entire island would have

A group of Easter Islanders employed on Brander's plantations. Their descendants occupy a district in Papeete, Tahiti, today.

Opposite: Bavarian missionary Father Sebastian Englert settled on Easter Island in 1935 and lived there until his death in 1969. Passionately interested in the island's culture, he published his studies in a book called *La Tierra de Hotu Matua* (The Land of Hotu Matua).

been deserted if Dutrou-Bornier had not intervened and forced a hundred islanders to stay behind. In 1877 he was mysteriously assassinated.

Numerous ships then called at the island, including an American vessel, the USS *Mohican*, which anchored there from 18 to 30 December 1886. It was during this short stay that William Thomson carried out the first archaeological and ethnographic investigations. A house in the ceremonial village of Orongo was destroyed to extract its painted slabs.

Annexation by Chile in 1888

After Dutrou-Bornier's death, Brander employed Alexander Salmon as manager of his affairs on the island. The son of an important merchant from Tahiti and of Ariitaimai, the Tahitian princess, Salmon was to live on the island for almost twenty years with a team of Tahitians. He got on well with the Easter Islanders and helped to improve their living conditions. The island's economy developed rapidly through a massive introduction of livestock.

In 1888 the Chilean government bought the land belonging to Brander's son. Chile acquired all the territory except for the village of Hanga Roa and the surrounding area, which remained the property of the islanders. Captain Policarpo Toro annexed the island on 9 September 1888. In 1901 its control devolved to the navy. In 1966 a Chilean decree created a new department: Easter Island, province of Valparaíso.

A Chilean postage stamp depicting a *moai* from Easter Island.

A Tahitian legend relates: "So Tane set off again in his canoe, he sailed from generation to generation and continued to sail from generation to generation! They reached an abyss in the east, and an abyss in the west. They crossed regions with violent tides and regions with light breezes. The canoe was carried here and there in opposing currents."

CHAPTER II
CATAMARANS BENEATH THE STARS

The Polynesians have sometimes been compared to the Vikings. In fact, their epic story of seafaring covers a much vaster expanse of ocean (two of their boats, opposite); they traveled from New Zealand to Hawaii and Easter Island. Right: A 19th-century engraving of a Polynesian.

At an early stage in prehistoric times, people started to venture far from the Pacific coasts. In Japan traces of sea craft have been discovered in sites of the Jomon culture dating from the 5th millennium BC. In northern Melanesia evidence of even earlier great navigations has been found: Around 5500 BC maritime populations were already trading in precious obsidian. A few centuries later, New Caledonia was reached. These seafarers were probably still very far from our ancient Easter Islanders.

Around 1500 BC Sea Peoples Crossed the Western Pacific in Search of New Lands

Several centuries before the start of the Christian era, they reached eastern Polynesia after some incredible crossings. Although it is still not possible to date these voyages with any precision, these sailors were certainly present in the Marquesas about 150 BC, and in Hawaii and Easter Island around AD 500. From the Society Islands one of their last great voyages of colonization would bring them to New Zealand around AD 800.

Before their dispersal they had probably reached the Peruvian coast, on the other side of the Pacific—from where they brought back the sweet potato, which was later introduced, under the name *kumara*, within a "Polynesian triangle" measuring seven thousand miles on each side.

COLONIZATION DATES OF THE ISLANDS OF OCEANIA

CHINA

BC

SUMATRA

JA

toward Madagascar

Indian Ocean

Skeletons of a Maori chief and of a moa. This giant bird, which had disappeared from New Zealand before 1500 BC, left enduring memories in oral traditions.

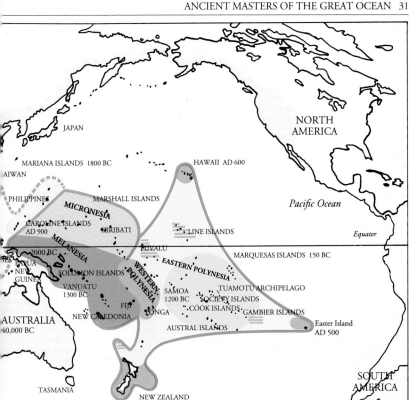

These sea peoples brought the plants necessary for their food, care, and clothes, along with certain trees needed for their utilitarian and symbolic functions. The taro, the yam, the sweet potato, and the banana were thus introduced to the new lands. They also transported their familiar animals from island to island: pigs, dogs, chickens, rats, and small birds with colored plumage, emissaries of the divine powers. The colonizing ancestors of the archipelagos could therefore legitimately be considered as gods, who were the origin of everything in nature indispensable to people.

The "masters of the sea" sailed around the western Pacific 3500 years ago, carrying from island to island a type of pottery known as *Lapita* with characteristic ornamentation and shapes (opposite above). These sailors are called Protopolynesians; they reached the islands of Tonga and Samoa around 1000 or 1200 BC.

The Great Eastward Adventure: Little by Little the Expedition Fleets Populated the Pacific

The ancestors of the Polynesians started traveling from Indonesia along the eastern coast of New Guinea; then they occupied the shores of the islands of Melanesia and headed out to the east. They populated lands at distances of 250 to 375 miles away, as far as the archipelagos of Tonga and Samoa. Next they had to cross a gap of about a thousand miles between these lands and the Society Islands, with a possible stop, around halfway across, in the Cook Islands. They then reached present-day French Polynesia.

On 14 May 1774 Cook witnessed the full splendor of Polynesian naval power: An armada of 160 vessels was assembled in Matavai Bay, Tahiti.

The first Europeans in the South Pacific were fascinated by the Polynesians' nautical talents and the qualities of their boats. They were amazed to find that vessels a hundred feet long could be created with simple stone tools.

For their transoceanic trips, the Melanesians and Polynesians had built huge expedition catamarans, whose two hulls, joined by a bridge, carried sails and a solid shelter. These boats no longer existed when the Europeans discovered the remote Pacific Islands. The most regular voyages, which went no farther than 250 miles, were by then

The painter William Hodges immortalized this scene, transposing it to the island of Raiatéa. One can see double-hulled vessels, 55 to 110 feet long, which could carry from 30 to 300 warriors. Their carved bows might rise 33 feet above the water.

restricted to contacts within the same archipelago. At the end of the 18th century, the most imposing vessels were those intended for the gods and for war.

Large dismasted double-hulled boat (above left) in its hangar on Tonga.

Through Maori Chants, Testimony about These Ancient Expeditions Has Come Down to Us

In each archipelago, oral traditions have left us accounts intended to legitimize the land rights of certain lineages that are recognized as the first occupants of the territory. These accounts are often enriched with concrete details about the adventures involved in the voyage and landing. In this way we know of the voyage that brought

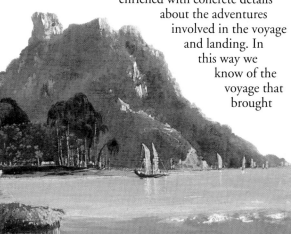

The big Polynesian boats were made of planks cut with stone adzes; the edges of these planks were pierced with chisels of human bone or shell. They were then assembled on the keel and framework by "sewing" them edge to edge with strong ropes made of braided coconut fiber. The joints were caulked with coconut-fiber tow and the sticky sap of the breadfruit tree.

Above: View of Matavai Bay, Tahiti.

Left: Part of the port of Fare on Huahiné.

King Ngahue of Tahiti to New Zealand in the year 800 or 900, centuries after the colonization of Easter Island. His fleet was made up of six vessels, plus the *Arawa* (shark), the flagship. Each ship carried 140 people. The Maori chants tell us the names of the chiefs of the fleet, and they also describe the setting up of the sacred places, how the different chiefs took possession of the ground, and the voyages of exploration along the coasts.

Below: Only very small boats were found on Easter Island (bottom pair) when Jacob Roggeveen arrived. However, these frail craft resembled other Polynesian canoes (upper pair, from the Tuamotu archipelago).

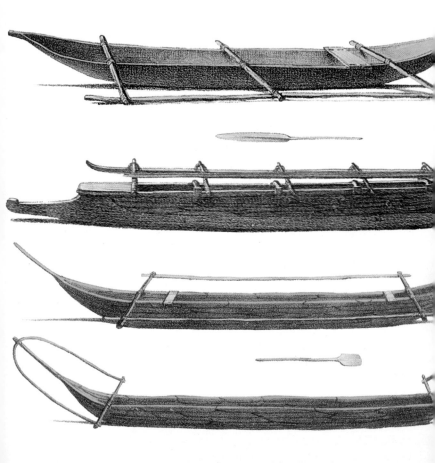

The Polynesians, Masters of the Great Ocean, Had Excellent Knowledge of the Winds

In order to sail over such great distances, one needed not only huge, robust vessels and a daring born of solid traditions, but also a perfect knowledge of the winds, currents, the way to steer, and favorable meteorological conditions. The first of these conditions had already been achieved by the sea peoples for thousands of years when, leaving western Polynesia, they launched their catamarans toward the east. Knowledge of the rotation of the heavenly bodies enabled them to name an archipelago after the stars that shone successively at its zenith; they then strove to maintain their route along the axis joining the island of departure's star to the destination's star.

The Polynesians constantly advanced eastward, which usually meant going against the direction of winds and dominant currents. However, there are times during the year when the winds blow from west to east for a week or two. Also, meteorological conditions are perpetually evolving, and it is not impossible that winds in the past might in fact have settled into a fairly durable west–east pattern, which would have further encouraged sailors to try their luck toward the east.

The distance that could be covered in ten days of constant wind was considerable. In 1976 the *Hokulea*, a catamaran that was a reproduction of ancient Polynesian boats, traveled from Hawaii to Tahiti (2800 miles), with wind abeam, in thirty-five days. The pilots used traditional navigational methods, steering only by the sun and stars.

The performance of the *Hokulea* coincides with the range attributed by Captain Cook to the Tahitian catamarans; theoretically it means Easter Island is twelve days from the "nearby" Gambier Islands.

Island Dust

Although there are thousands of islands, atolls, and reefs in the South Pacific, the surface area of land above the water is extremely small. The chances of encountering an island are minute if one relies on luck alone.

This 1792 painting illustrates the main types of vessels used by the Polynesians: The double-hulled canoe; the canoe used for fishing and trips in the lagoon, which had a balancing outrigger but no sail; the canoe with sail and outrigger; and the double canoe with sail for interisland trips.

A Unique Race

"It is extraordinary that the same nation should have spread themselves over all the isles in this vast ocean, from New Zealand to this island, which is almost one-fourth part of the circumference of the Globe. Many of them have now no other knowledge of each other, than what is preserved by antiquated tradition; and they have, by length of time, become, as it were, different nations, each having adopted some peculiar custom or habit, etc. Nevertheless, a careful observer will soon see the affinity each has to the other."

James Cook,
A Voyage Towards the South Pole, and Round the World...in the Years 1772–1775, Vol. I, 1777

A late-18th-century view of a bay in Tahiti.

Between the Hawaiian Archipelago, New Zealand, and Easter Island: The Great Polynesian Family

During their quest for the southern continent, Westerners soon noticed that wherever they landed in the Pacific they found themselves among peoples with a similar appearance, related customs, and the same—or a closely related—language. The Tahitians accompanying Captain Cook could easily communicate with the Marquesans, but also— albeit with a little more difficulty—with the Maori of New Zealand and the Easter Islanders. It was in Tahitian that the Reverend William Ellis preached in Hawaii in 1823, and the missionaries would address the Easter Islanders in this language as well.

The Polynesians' similarity was apparent not only in their conception of the world and their way of honoring their gods, naming kings, and treating their dead, but also in the way they built their houses and adorned and fed themselves. Hence, in every place, birds and divinities were closely associated, and *mana* was the name for power par excellence—hundreds of gods, among whom Tangaroa seems the most important, were invested with this power. His creatures, Tiki, the masculine principle, and Hina, his female complement, were at the origin of the human race.

The Polynesians, People of the Sea, Displayed a Powerful Attachment to the Land

Throughout the Great Ocean, the Polynesians have a fond regard for the products of an earth that can accommodate fragile breadfruit tree saplings, banana shoots, taro, yam,

A New Zealand Maori, a Hawaiian, and an Easter Islander share the same extended conception of the family —a family to which adoption can add new members who enjoy the same land rights as the biological heirs.

Below left: Tu, king of Tahiti.

sweet potato, sugarcane, arrowroot, and palm lily.

On almost every island, there is a Polynesian fable concerning a dog, a pig, a chicken, and a rat. These companions were always present during great voyages, but sometimes did not survive them, or proved to be too much competition in lands with little food.

Finally, Polynesian equipment and techniques were everywhere born out of opportunism and out of situations of scarcity encountered on atolls where the only raw materials that could be transformed into tools were provided by the animal kingdom: shells, teeth, and bones. Artifacts such as stone tools, fishhooks, and tattooing combs show typically Polynesian features and were barely affected by local particularities.

On Easter Island, a small group of settlers was to develop—against a Polynesian background— a few features that were exacerbated by isolation.

The members of the Polynesian family are intimately linked by ceremonial monuments and families' rights to the land, by the method of dividing the land among the individuals who make up society, and by the names of the elementary territorial divisions.

Below: Matavai Bay, Tahiti.

An Easter Island myth gives the following account: "A priestess had landed on the islet of Motiro Hiva. The gods Make Make and Haua brought her their catch of fish. One day, Make Make said: 'I came here in search of birds. Why don't we drive them in front of us as far as Easter Island?' Haua replied: 'Fine. Order the old priestess to get ready because we're going to leave for Easter Island.'"

CHAPTER III
EARLY LIFE ON EASTER ISLAND

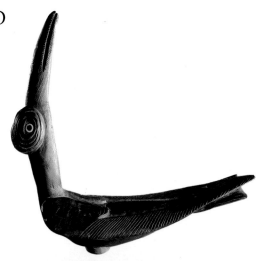

The Easter Islanders' life was punctuated by the ceremonies of the birdman cult.

Left: Pierre Loti's imaginary depiction of Easter Islanders. Right: A wooden sculpture of a bird.

The King Was of Divine Ancestry and Was Responsible for Relations with the Gods

On Easter Island the king's civil authority depended on his *mana*, the small scrap of divine power that he inherited from his ancestors. It was thanks to the presence of the king, "dripping" with *mana*, that the territory in his charge was spared catastrophes, that migratory birds and turtles appeared at the right moments, and that domestic animals, vegetables, and fruits grew in abundance. It was also the king, the *ariki mau*, who in times of drought, armed with a long baton, begged the god Hiro to bring rain, who declared a taboo on cultivation, or who lifted this ban and authorized harvests. The first fruits of all the island's products were offered to him, and he alone had the right to disobey taboos and eat tuna in winter! The sovereign's *mana* benefited the community but was dangerous for individuals: He could not be approached with impunity, and mortals would not dare to watch him or his heir eating or even sleeping.

The sacred royal residence was at Anakena. It was there that, wearing six small wooden pectoral ornaments (the *rei miro*) around his neck and holding his scepter (*ua*) in his hand, he regularly received the homage of the tribal representatives. Festivals were organized for him

The wooden insignia that adorned the king during festivities were finely worked: The *ua* (left and detail below) was decorated with a carved head, and the ends of the *rei miro* represented bearded figures or cockerels.

to judge the quality of young people's tattoos and ear ornaments. Accompanied by a priest, he had to eat a meal in every newly constructed house. He also inaugurated new boats and baptized twins with a royal name.

A Very Hierarchical Society

The king of Easter Island was always born of the Honga clan, whose members—descendants of the eldest son of Hotu Matua who, according to legend, was the first to land on the island—were the island's nobility.

The priests enjoyed prerogatives close to those of the nobles, but political power was in the hands of the *mata toa*, the war chiefs. Specialists—chanters, sculptors, fishermen—were held in an esteem that varied according to their specialty and their skill.

The common people, who were in the majority, cultivated the land and

"We can catch no glimpse of relations between individuals save the exterior forms and tokens of politeness.... When a chief paid a visit to the chief of another tribe he was met along the road by groups of warriors, who formed an escort. On these occasions no doubt the chanters recited long genealogies, as is still done on the Tuamotus. The two chiefs advanced to meet and pressed the wings of their noses together."
Alfred Métraux
Easter Island, 1957

A man and a woman from Easter Island.

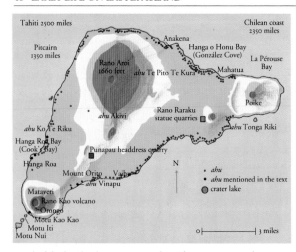

The principal sites on Easter Island.

probably built the great works. Slaves captured during fights were forced into hard labor. Sometimes destined for sacrifice, they were considered by their masters to be a tasty food reserve.

The Division of Land Was Derived from Hotu Matua's Six Sons

According to a traditional song, Hotu Matua had six sons, and he divided the island among them shortly before his death. Following the Polynesian rule, his eldest received the title of king together with the lands where his father had settled, around the bay of Anakena and to the northwest of it. His brothers occupied territories whose importance and location corresponded to their order of birth. This is how tradition explained the creation of six principal districts, or *mata*, probably symbolized by the six *rei miro* that the king wore during ceremonies.

Some of these domains were later subdivided. When the Europeans arrived, there were ten *mata* grouped into large rival entities: one to the east, the "small district," and the other to the west, the "large district." This division was also found in the ceremonial village of Orongo.

The Houses Were Grouped Under the Protective Gaze of the Sanctuary Gods

Each *mata* was made up of numerous lineages, or "families" in the broad sense, born of a common ancestor. Each lineage had an *ahu*, a place for ritual and burial erected by the family group, on which were set the *moai*, statues of its gods and its deified ancestors.

The *ahu* expressed the power and prestige of each family. The lineage's houses were grouped in front of this monument. Every hereditary domain was divided into *kainga*, parcels of land divided among the households. These were probably narrow strips of land stretching from the beach to the island's interior.

Map of the principal territorial divisions of Easter Island, drawn up in 1870.

Below: Entrance to an old chief's house.

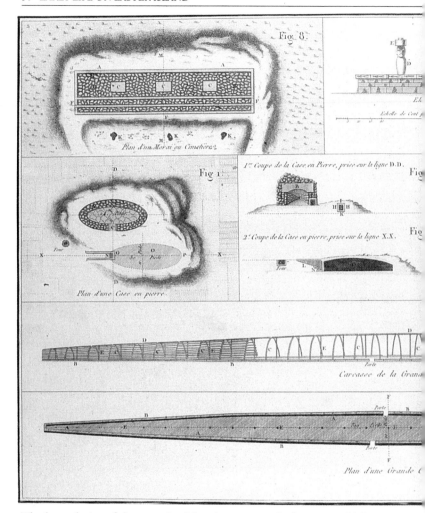

Fig. 8.

Plan d'un Morai ou Cimetière.

Échelle de Cent p

1.ᵉ Coupe de la Case en Pierre, prise sur la ligne D.D. Fig.

Fig. 1.

2.ᵉ Coupe de la Case en pierre, prise sur la ligne X.X. Fig.

Plan d'une Case en pierre.

Carcasse de la Grand

Plan d'une Grande C

The boundaries of these territorial units were marked by natural features (such as hills) or by monuments (*moais* and heaps of stones painted white). The distribution of the *mata* and their subdivisions resembled a sometimes incoherent-seeming mosaic, because each group had to be able to reach the

View of different structures on the island, drawn by Bernizet and published in *Voyage Autour de Monde* in 1797.

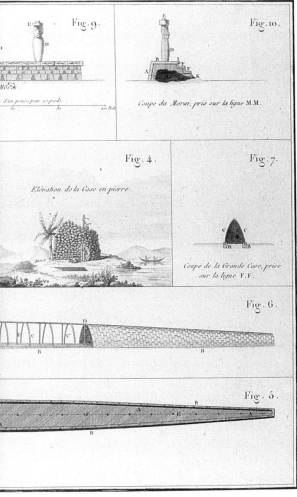

Fig. 9.

Fig. 10.

Coupe du Morai, prise sur la ligne M.M.

Fig. 4.

Fig. 7.

Elévation de la Case en pierre.

Coupe de la Grande Case, prise sur la ligne F.F.

Fig. 6.

Fig. 5.

The framework of the large house (figs. 5 and 6) was made up of arched rafters intersecting with both sides of a ridge-purlin to which they were solidly attached. The ridge was supported by numerous poles. Purlins, fixed horizontally on the rafters, permitted the attachment of the roofing components.

beaches or cave refuges without coming under the law of another; they needed to procure reeds from the base of the volcanoes for roofing, obtain the precious obsidian of Mount Orito and the andesite of Mount Otu for weapons and tools, and open up quarries in the slopes of Rano Raraku.

The Roofs of Their Dwellings Rested Directly on the Ground

The traditional dwelling that is best known—because it was copiously described by Western voyagers—is an elongated, elliptical structure, often compared to an upturned boat. The biggest of these houses could be three hundred feet in length; the one visited by La Pérouse's expedition sheltered two hundred people.

The roofs were covered with matting, sugarcane leaves, bundles of rushes or grass. The low, narrow door was in the middle of the facade; statuettes or wooden sculptures might be placed in a kind of small vestibule to protect the entrance. According to tradition, the hut's central post was endowed with magical powers. The door was closed by a net whose mesh was small enough to prevent chickens from getting through.

The Easter Islanders were accustomed to gathering on a semicircular paved area in front of the house, where they worked, ate, and chatted during the day. At night the members of the household slept on rush mats laid on a thick mattress of grass, their heads resting on stone pillows that were often decorated.

Some architectural features differed according to the social class of the inhabitant: The dwellings of the chiefs, dignitaries, priests, and nobles were distinguished by an entrance fitted with a vestibule and by a well-laid-out path made of stones in parallel rows.

This type of wooden figurine, called *moko*, representing a lizard, was placed at the entrance of houses.

The Islanders Sometimes Lived in the Island's Numerous Caves

The Easter Islanders fitted out natural cavities to serve as dwellings. The entrance might be walled up, leaving only a narrow passage through which one had to crawl. Inside, the sleeping area could be set up on a stone platform. Small, unconverted caves were used as temporary dwellings, and others were used as hiding places in times of war. Taboo refuges were set up in lava tubes; the underground chamber was reached through a narrow artificial passage. These underground refuges were sometimes decorated with petroglyphs.

The *Hare Moa*, or Chicken Houses

About sixty feet from the dwellings there were stone constructions, rectangular or sometimes circular in shape, made of small stones that were piled up and carefully fitted.

Inside, along the length of the center of the structure, there were small chambers reached by a narrow passage. A small opening, at ground level, could be closed with a single large stone.

At night the Easter Islanders shut their chickens into these constructions as a precaution against theft, which was common on the island. The birds represented wealth for their owner, not only because of their eggs and flesh but also because they were offered as gifts during ceremonies and festivals, and these exchanges were a fundamental part of social life on the island.

A fanciful represen-tation of an Easter Island woman with a basket of fish (above) and a chicken house (left).

Fishing Was Hazardous and Scarcely Made Up for the Shortage of Meat Resources

Nobody knows if the first Easter Islanders brought their dogs and their pigs with them when they migrated; no bones of these animals have yet been found in the oldest archaeological layers. So chickens, rats, and seabirds constituted the only usual meat resources from the land. Cannibal meals were reserved for military chiefs and their warriors. Protein intake was therefore rare. Fishing from land or in boats brought food from the sea to diversify and enhance a largely vegetable diet, based above all on the inevitable sweet potato.

The most common type of fishing was carried out by women among the rocks on the shore; they caught small fish and crabs with a harpoon, and they gathered sea urchins and various species of shellfish. At night the men captured crayfish and octopi in nets, or by hand, by the light of torches.

The Easter Islanders' fishing fleet was very small. Roggeveen said he saw several canoes in 1722, and Cook would count no more than three or four in 1774.

Aboard these canoes of "sewn" planks, the specialist fishermen headed off the coast, guided by landmarks which in some cases were statues. But Easter Island is not protected by a coral reef, and the heavy sea made fishing there dangerous, if not impossible, during the late winter months of July to September. In any case, it was forbidden by a taboo during that season. Only the royal canoe, in which dignitaries were the sole people allowed to sit, could venture far from the coast during this time of the year.

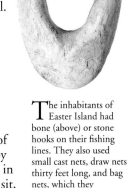

The inhabitants of Easter Island had bone (above) or stone hooks on their fishing lines. They also used small cast nets, draw nets thirty feet long, and bag nets, which they submerged to a depth of more than 150 feet.

The Underground Gardens Sheltered Crops from the Wind and Sun

The inhabitants of Easter Island built small stone structures called *manavai* to retain soil humidity and to protect the crops from the heat of the sun as well as the violent salt winds. These constructions were generally set up close to the dwellings, and were made of thick stone walls enclosing areas of about ten to thirty feet in diameter, in which vegetables, paper mulberries, and bananas were planted. These gardens were isolated or

The Easter Islanders cultivated some of their fruits and vegetables in deposits of wet humus that accumulated in naturally collapsed lava tubes.

The sweet potato, of South American origin, constituted one of the staple foods.

assembled in groups of up to forty enclosures. Collapsed lava tubes were also used; sweet potatoes, yams, arrowroot, taro, palm lilies, sugarcane, and other plants thus grew in a veritable greenhouse, sometimes fifteen or twenty feet deep, and sheltered from the elements. These gardens were often bounded by a small rectangular or circular wall. According to the first European visitors, people also cultivated fields that were laid out in unenclosed rectangular strips, protected from the elements by a mass of grass that preserved the humidity and served as fertilizer.

Garments of Grass and Beaten Bark

The *mahute* or paper mulberry, cultivated close to the dwellings in the *manavai*, was used for making *tapa*, a material of beaten bark.

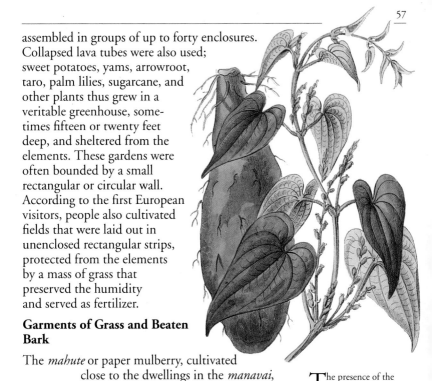

The presence of the yam (above) and arrowroot (below) in the Pacific Islands marks the Polynesians' route from southeast Asia.

The women were responsible for making this plant cloth. As in other parts of Polynesia, the bark was detached from the young trunks,

soaked to make it supple, and then pounded on a square stone anvil with a stone or a beater made of a quadrangular-sectioned piece of toromiro wood. After being dried for several days between banana leaves, the beaten bark cloths were sewn together with a bird-bone needle.

Not much *mahute* bark was produced on the island, and it was difficult to make cloth, so the Easter Islanders wore few garments, sometimes reduced to their simplest expression.

Men and young people wore a narrow strip of *tapa* by way of a G-string, which they very often replaced with a simple tuft of grass fixed to a string of human hair. Women also wore this type of decorated belt, sometimes covered with a rectangle of *tapa* that they wrapped around their hips like a skirt.

The most remarkable garment was a kind of cape called a *kahu*, which men and women threw around their shoulders and which covered their

Early-19th-century illustrators interpreted the texts concerned with voyages of discovery very freely. In this fanciful illustration (above), there are only two things that actually come from Easter Island: the *ua* baton resting on the man's shoulder, and the figures' elongated earlobes.

backs. These coats were made of small quilts of *tapa* sewn together and dyed yellow or orange. The size of these garments varied according to social class: The dignitaries and kings wore elegantly colored and very finely made *kahu*s, which came down to the knees.

Each act of everyday life—eating a meal, making a tool, launching a boat, inaugurating a house—was accompanied by a short propitiatory prayer, a gesture of blessing, or a ritual devoted to a particular god. The prayers of ordinary mortals sufficed for commonplace acts, but for consecrations needing a strong dose of *mana*, one called on the king and the priests who lived in the shadow of the divinities.

Men and women wore tattoos indicating their social status. Women were more discreet.

Make Make, Supreme God of Easter Island

Tangaroa, the god who was the origin of everything in Polynesia, appears only discreetly in Easter Island's traditions. The main divinity was Make Make, who does not exist anywhere else in Polynesia. He was the guardian protector of Hotu Matua's clan, raised to the status of first god in the island's pantheon.

However, Make Make seems to come straight out of the original egg of Tangaroa. The depictions of him as a human being with a bird's head evoke the myth of how Tangaroa created the world: For millions of years Tangaroa remained in the darkness. Existing before the world, he had created himself and given himself a name. His shell was like an egg spinning in infinite space, with no sky, no earth, no

Pierre Loti drew faithful reproductions of Easter Island's landscapes and monuments, including the one below left of the east coast between Vaihu and Rano Raraku. But he also drew works of pure fiction, like this ceremony below right before the same *ahu*, in which he tried to re-create the atmosphere of the ancient cults.

sea, no moon, no sun, and no stars. When he broke his shell, he got rid of the feathers that covered his body; they fell to earth and gave birth to vegetation. The myth of the original egg holds a primordial place in the mythology of Easter Island.

Make Make is also depicted by two big eyes, like those in a skull. Human sacrifices and the first fruits of the harvests were offered to him, as well as to his companion Haua.

Lizard Woman and Gannet Woman Taught Humans the Art of Tattooing

Make Make is the creator of human beings: He brought them forth from the ground like plants. By masturbating in the earth he gave birth to some of the first gods in the Easter Island pantheon—Tive, Rorai, Hova, and the old woman Arangi Kote Kote.

There was a considerable host of minor divinities, the *akuaku*. They could be incarnated in living beings and materialized in the form of objects or natural phenomena: Te Emu was a landslide, and Mata Vara Vara was large raindrops. From them came certain techniques: tattooing, dyeing with turmeric (taught by two female demons, Lizard Woman and Gannet Woman), and the manufacture of bone fishhooks.

Two generations after the conversion to Christianity, the islanders could still recall ninety gods. By 1935, in the third generation, ethnologist Alfred Métraux listed only thirty.

These gods resided in the territories of different clans. Most of them were probably divine protectors of the families, to which they transmitted messages from the next world in the form of omens. People never forgot to present them with food offerings every time an oven was opened.

After Having Surprised the Gods in Their Sleep, Chief Tuu Ko Ihu Carved the First Wooden Statuettes in Their Image

Despite the scarcity of trees, there is an extremely rich and astonishingly diverse collection of wooden sculpture on the island. Its originality is expressed particularly in the *moai kava kava* statuettes, which represent emaciated beings with prominent rib cages and spines. For the most part they are clearly male, with artificially lengthened earlobes, in accordance with tradition. The black obsidian of the pupils, accentuated by a white circle of bone or shell, gives them a worryingly intense gaze. Motifs in the form of birds or anthropomorphic monsters sometimes decorate the top of the skull. According to the traditions collected in the second half of the 19th century, these statuettes represented secondary divinities, each family's household gods. They also depicted the corpse of a chief or an important person who had advanced to the rank of protective spirit.

The islanders were proud of possessing several of these little sculptures. During festivals, at harvest time, or when offering the first fruits, people would decorate themselves by hanging them from their bodies on fine cords, and then they would dance. Some would parade and spin around with ten or twenty statuettes! These objects were carefully kept in the dwellings, and when they were removed from their

The numerous wooden *moai kava kava* statuettes (below) from Easter Island are almost as famous as the giant statues. On the other hand, there are only three figurines in the whole world that are made of a reed skeleton covered by *tapa*; one is opposite. They are painted with polychrome designs that imitate tattoos, and their function remains unknown.

protective wrapping, the Easter Islanders recited incantations while rocking them like infants. Often carved in toromiro wood, the statuettes were probably the temporary receptacles of the gods and ancestral spirits. As in other parts of Polynesia, they became sacred only when the invoked spirit occupied the sculpture, after incantations had been used as prayers. Flat female images—the *moai papa*—as well as fish, turtles, chickens, rats, and lizards were also carved in wood.

In 1868 an Old Piece of Wood Revealed the Existence of an Unknown Script

As a mark of respect, in 1868 the newly converted Easter Islanders handed over to Bishop Tepano Jaussen a long cord braided with their hair that had been wrapped around an old piece of wood. After examining his present, Tepano Jaussen looked under the cord and noticed that the small plank was covered with hieroglyphs. The first *kohau rongo rongo* (chanter's staff) tablet had been discovered.

In 1864 Eugène Eyraud had already pointed out that "in all their houses one can find tablets of wood or sticks covered with many kinds of hieroglyphic signs: figures of animals unknown on the island, which the people trace by means of sharp stones. Each figure has its own name."

The *Kohau Rongo Rongo* Tablets Still Have Not Given Up Their Secrets

The antiquity of this "script" has been greatly disputed. According to tradition, it was Hotu Matua who created the first schools for teaching these tablets. But some specialists believe this writing was a recent invention, inspired by the treaty signed with the Spaniards in 1770.

There is little ancient information about the script's meaning or the way in which the Easter Islanders used the twenty-one authentic tablets that have been collected, together with a staff and three or four pectorals bearing identical glyphs.

Both sides of the tablets are covered with geometric, anthropomorphic, and zoomorphic characters, arranged in regular lines. Each tablet bears the same signs, some of which may be combined. The "reading" was carried out from top to bottom, and from left to right. As the signs are inverted on every other line, the reciter had to turn the tablet at the end of each line. This writing is unique in the world. So far all

The glyphs on the tablets represent animals and plants of the local flora, ordinary objects, parts of the human body, and geometric designs. On the twenty-one known tablets and the five royal insignia, there are 14,021 signs, including 595 basic signs.

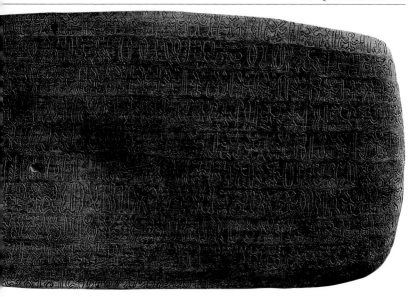

attempts to decipher it have been unsuccessful. In fact, even if certain signs may represent words, there is no proof that complete sentences or a grammar exist; it is believed that these glyphs served as mnemonics to facilitate the reciting of oral traditions and genealogies.

The 1135 signs on the *aruku kurenga* tablet were engraved with shark teeth or obsidian flakes. The sooty tern, incarnation of the god Make Make, is represented 183 times here.

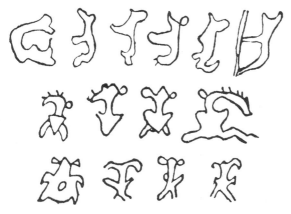

Every Year the Disciples of the *Tangata Rongo Rongo* Gather at Anakena

Birds painted on the ceiling of the cave of Ana Kai Tangata (below and below left).

The tablets were associated with chants intoned by specialists, the *tangata rongo rongo*, who, together with their servants, were the only people allowed to handle these taboo objects.

There were different kinds of tablets for chants during festivals, war, and funeral ceremonies. The disciples of the *tangata rongo rongo* were taught to write and read the tablets in special schools that existed in all districts of the island, the most famous at Anakena.

Here, once a year, the king presided over a public ceremony during which the *tangata rongo rongo* competed in tests that involved reciting sacred tablets. These experts then presented their pupils. If one of them faltered in deciphering the glyphs, the tablets were taken away from his master. This very popular gathering attracted spectators from every area.

During less grandiose ceremonies, at the new moon and its last quarter, the king inspected the tablets. The *tangata rongo rongo* also gathered once a year at Orongo to recite the sacred chants during the birdman festival.

The Birdman Cult: Heroes Became Kings

Easter Island's greatest religious festival was the *tangata manu*—the birdman—ceremony, which took place every year at the beginning of the southern spring, in Orongo.

The choice of this site is explained by its proximity to the three islets of Motu Nui, Motu Iti, and Motu Kao Kao, the refuge to which Make Make himself had led the seabirds. It was on the largest of these islets, Motu Nui, that the migratory sooty terns came to lay their eggs. Unlike other festivals, this ceremony is relatively well known because it persisted well after the island's conversion.

Numerous petroglyphs are scattered around the island. In Orongo alone more than five hundred depictions of the birdman and the god Make Make have been recorded.

Below: Birds in a bas-relief at *ahu* Nau Nau at Anakena.

Inside the Crater of
Otuiti. Easter Island. 1868

"These Monstrous Faces"

"It was about an hour and a half after we recommenced our journey after the stop at Vaihu that we began to make out, upright on the side of this mountain, great figures that projected enormous shadows on to the dismal grass. They are not set up in any order and look toward us as though they want to know who is arriving, although we also noticed a few long profiles with pointed noses turned in other directions.... They have no body, they are merely colossal heads, emerging from the earth at the end of long necks and rising up as if to scan the far-off distance, which always remains motionless and empty. Which human race do they represent, with the tip of their noses raised and their thin lips jutting out in a pout of disdain or mockery? They have no eyes, nothing but deep cavities beneath their foreheads, under the vast and noble arch of their eyebrows—and yet they appear to look and to think."

Pierre Loti
L'Ile de Pâques, 1872

Inside the crater of Rano Raraku, depicted by Linton Palmer in 1868.

Huts of Images.
Easter 9th

"The Monumental Crowns"

"Mention must…be made of the crowns or hats which adorned the figures on the *ahu*.… These coverings for the head were cylindrical in form, the bottom being slightly hollowed out into an oval depression in order to fit on to the head of the image.… The top was worked into a boss or knot. The material is a red volcanic tuff found in a small crater on the side of a larger volcano, generally known as Punapau, not far from Cook's Bay.… In the crater itself are the old quarries. A few half-buried hats may be seen there, and the path up to it, and for some hundreds of yards from the foot of the mountain, is strewn with them. They are at this stage simply large cylinders, from four feet to eight feet high, from six feet to nine feet across."

Katherine Routledge,
The Mystery of Easter Island, 1919

Group of *pukao*, or stone headdresses, on the edge of the Punapau quarry, depicted by Linton Palmer in 1868.

It consisted of an organized competition, a quest for the first sooty tern egg on the islet of Motu Nui. This ritual, closely linked to the cult of the god Make Make, had important social implications. Only the *mata toa* (the principal war chiefs) could aspire to the title of birdman. The candidates were appointed by the priests who had received this revelation in a dream. The war chiefs could participate in the ordeal themselves, or entrust the task of finding the first egg to their servants, called *hopu.*

"In colour, features, and language they bear such affinity to the people of the more western isles, that no one will doubt but that they have had the same origin."
James Cook,
A Voyage Towards the South Pole, and Round the World...in the Years 1772–1775, Vol. I, 1777

The Men, Whose Faces Were Painted Red and Black and Whose Heads Were Decorated with Feathers, Set Out for Orongo, Brandishing Dancing Oars

Below: Engraving of Easter Islanders, c. 1820.

The ceremony began in July. The participants left their families and their village and settled at Mataveri, in the island's southwest corner, at the foot of Rano Kao volcano. They stayed there while they prepared the accessories and ornaments that were indispensable for the numerous ceremonies, and lived in big huts built for this purpose. (Mataveri is also associated with cannibal feasts.)

Then the men left Mataveri in their ceremonial costumes and followed the path called the "road of the *ao,*" which led to the ceremonial village of Orongo. This village, comprised of about fifty houses built of slabs of rock, stands on the rim of Rano Kao, on the last remnant of the volcano's southern side, which has been partly eroded by the ocean. It leads to a group of basalt slabs on which countless birdman figures have been carved.

To Reach Motu Nui, the Servants Braved a Shark-Infested Sea

In late August the men left Orongo for Motu Nui. This trial put their physical prowess and moral courage to the test because it involved swimming to the islet through shark-infested waters. The swimmers used conical floats of rushes, inside of which they carried provisions in anticipation of a long stay. After settling into the islet's little caves, they were provided with fresh supplies, if the weather permitted, by relatives or their master's servants.

While the competitors were looking for the first egg to be laid by the sooty terns, many ceremonies were taking place at Orongo to gain the favor of the divinities. People danced in front of the houses, and by night and day the *tangata rongo rongo* recited rhythmic chants in the stone house containing the sacred statue of *Hoa haka nana ia* (the "Stolen Friend"), while offerings were presented to the gods Make Make and Haua. In September, the servants redoubled their vigilance. They slept little, scrutinizing the sky for days, while reciting prayers. The one who found the first speckled egg on

"It is indisputable that these people are Polynesians, Maori. Although they have become a little paler than their ancestors because of the cloudy climate, they have retained their fine stature, the very typical beautiful face, a long oval in shape, with big eyes placed close together. They have also kept several of the customs of their brothers over there, and in particular they speak their language."

Pierre Loti
L'Île de Pâques, 1872

the grass sped to the rock known as the Bird's Cry and yelled the name of the victor (his employer), telling him to shave his head. This cry was heard by the lookout posted in a cave in the Orongo cliff. The servant would then rush back to the village, safe from danger, since the swimmer was now supposed to be protected by the egg's magical powers and by the gods.

Considered To Be the God's Very Incarnation, the Birdman Was a Sacred Individual

The servant then handed the sacred egg to his master, who had shaved his head, eyebrows, and eyelashes and covered his face in red and black marks. The new birdman went down to Mataveri at the head of a tumultuous procession with a wooden bird attached to his back. There was a succession of dances and chants, and human victims, picked out by the priests or by the birdman himself, were sacrificed to the god Make Make. The crowd would become tense, and quarrels would break out

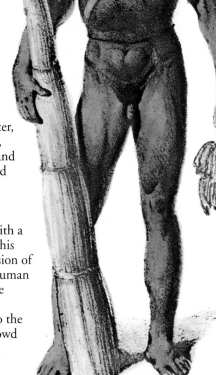

The *hopu*, depicted here with his float of rushes, was supposed to have no free will. He was merely an intermediary through whom Make Make made known the person he had chosen to become birdman.

Hundreds of birdman figures are engraved on these basalt blocks located at the end of the village of Orongo, at a spot called Mata Ngarau, from which one can see the islets of Motu Nui and Motu Iti and the pointed rock of Motu Kao Kao to the right.

"There is no orderly arrangement in the way these petroglyphs are grouped and it would be vain to seek any overall plan. They are the products of isolated efforts on the part of generations of devout worshipers, who, by this pious labor, sought either to win the favor of the bird god or to thank him for his aid after victory."
Alfred Métraux
Easter Island, 1957

Opposite left: Ovoid red stone from *ahu* Te Pito Te Kura.

until the new birdman of the year departed; he withdrew to a house at the foot of Rano Raraku, by the *ahu* Tonga Riki or other important *ahu.* He changed his name and gave the new year the name that had mysteriously been communicated to him by the gods in a dream.

Subject to very strict taboos, he could not leave his retreat; he was not permitted to bathe and had to refrain from sexual intercourse and eat only foods cooked in a special oven by a particular servant; he could not cut his hair or nails and, as a mark of distinction, wore a headdress made of human hair. The various tribes had to supply him with provisions. The sacred egg, supposed to bring abundance, was emptied, filled with *tapa,* and then suspended in the birdman's house.

Like the king, the birdman became a man-god. During his reign, he derived numerous political and economic advantages from his position. After a year, the magic egg lost its power. It was then thrown into the sea, hidden in a crack of rock at Rano Raraku, or preserved so that it could eventually be buried with the birdman in a hallowed place. The birdman left his retreat and returned to his previous occupation. For the rest of his life he enjoyed esteem and occupied a special place at festivals.

Ethnologist Alfred Métraux wrote: "During the three weeks we lived among these statues we saw them in sunshine, by moonlight, and on stormy nights. Each time we felt the same shock, the same uneasiness, as on the first day. This sense of oppression is due less to their dimensions than to their confused distribution."

CHAPTER IV
A THOUSAND GIGANTIC STATUES

Opposite: *Moai* at the foot of Rano Raraku quarry depicted by Linton Palmer in 1868.

In 1978, archaeologist Sergio Rapu, who was also the governor of Easter Island, discovered and reconstructed a statue's eye for the first time.

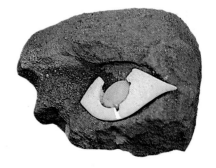

A Pedestal for the Gods: The *Ahu*

The term *ahu* designates a monumental structure, an open-air sanctuary erected in honor of the gods and deified ancestors. These sacred places, protected by a very strict prohibition, were political and religious centers. Each *ahu* belonged to an extended family or lineage. When the latter disappeared, as a result of war or epidemic, the monument was abandoned and its stones reused for other sanctuaries.

The architecture of these edifices reveals that they were rebuilt many times, reflecting the numerous political and social fluctuations that shook the island over time.

There are many of these often-spectacular sanctuaries on the island. In general, they are built on the coast, parallel to the shore, but some of them are placed so that they are perpendicular to the position of sunrise and sunset at the time of solstices and equinoxes.

This depiction of an *ahu* (left) is a lithograph illustrating an 1878 report on Easter Island by Alphonse Pinart, a French explorer. In fact, the statues were always placed on pedestals on top of the platform.

Stone Giants with Their Backs to the Sea

Big statues, the *moai*, carved out of the soft rocks of Rano Raraku volcano, stand on the sanctuary's platform; the number varies according to the importance of the monument. In general, the

medium-sized sanctuaries have five *moai*. The bonding of the supporting walls, often made up of enormous blocks remarkably fitted together, aroused Cook's admiration: "The workmanship is not inferior to the best plain piece of masonry we have in England. They use no sort of cement; yet the joints are exceedingly close, and the stones morticed and tenanted one into another, in a very artful manner."

Tombs are always associated with this structure. Behind certain *ahu* there are small rectangular stone structures or small mounds demarcated by lines of stones; these structures, crematoria, contain burned fragments of human bone. The *moai* of the *ahu* have their backs to the sea and face the lineage's houses.

William Hodges, the painter on James Cook's expedition, drew the quarries of Rano Raraku from memory, which explains certain inaccuracies, notably the depiction of *moai* with headdresses. In fact, only the statues on coastal *ahu* had headdresses.

"These platforms of masonry are… generally at the brink of the bank facing the sea, so that this face may be ten or twelve feet or more high, and the other may not be above three or four. They are built, or rather faced, with hewn stones of a very large size." This is how Cook described the sanctuaries of Easter Island. They are comparable to the *marae* of the Society Islands, the *tohua* of the Marquesas, and the *heiau* of the Hawaiian Islands.

Left: Easter Island depicted by William Hodges.

Science Fiction

The means of transporting these giants has been the subject of all sorts of hypotheses, some serious, others absurd. Erich Von Däniken can see no solution other than the intervention of extraterrestrials.

"The men who could execute such perfect work must have possessed ultra-modern tools.... A small group of intelligent beings was stranded on Easter Island owing to a 'technical hitch.' The stranded group had a great store of knowledge, very advanced weapons and a method of working stone unknown to us.... Perhaps to leave the natives a lasting memory of their stay, but perhaps also as a sign to the friends who were looking for them, the strangers extracted a colossal statue from the volcanic stone. Then they made more stone giants which they set up on stone pedestals along the coast so that they were visible from afar.... In the remote past there were intelligences with an advanced technology for whom the covering of vast distances in aircraft of the most varied kinds was no problem."

Erich Von Däniken
Return to the Stars
1972

> "These gloomy figures, these groups standing in the sunshine…quick, quick, I must sketch them in my album, since I have promised to do so, while my companions go to sleep in the grass. And my haste, my feverish haste to note down all these aspects—despite the fatigue and the urge to sleep against which I'm struggling—my haste is to enhance the strangeness and peculiarity of the memories that this vision will have left me."
>
> Pierre Loti
> *L'Ile de Pâques*, 1872

The *moai* dominate a vast esplanade where people gathered during community, social, and religious ceremonies. Several houses also stand facing the *ahu*. These were reserved for the chiefs, priests, and other dignitaries. The *ahu moai* are undeniably the most impressive and the most elaborate of these sanctuaries, veritable masterpieces of megalithic architecture.

Sanctuaries with Strange Shapes

There are also semipyramidal *ahu*. Smaller and far less elaborate than the *ahu moai*, they resemble low, flat-topped pyramids. Funerary chambers and cists are also installed in them; sometimes the dead were placed in the mass of stones, or in specially designed irregular holes. Some are surmounted by upright stones or fragments of old statues. Most of these monuments were built close to the ruins of an *ahu moai*, with materials taken from them. It is difficult to be sure whether all the semipyramidal *ahu* postdate the construction of the *ahu moai*. They could just as well be the prototypes of the big *ahu*.

The *ahu poepoe* owe their name to the fact that they resemble boats, their elongated raised extremities recalling the stern and bows of a ship. Close to Mahatua stands an *ahu poepoe* that is about two hundred feet in length. These *ahu* were generally built with selected stones that were well fitted but not carved.

Some statues on the slopes of Rano Raraku (below and opposite) were to be transported to the island's numerous *ahu*; others, set up on paved platforms, watched over the immense workshop where the statues were made. At present more than half of their height is buried by the slope's sediments.

Gods or Ancestors: Who Were the *Moai*?

Jacob Roggeveen was the first visitor to

express his surprise on seeing these giant sculptures. On this minute islet, lost in the middle of the ocean, hundreds of statues lay scattered at the foot of abandoned sanctuaries, and others were still imprisoned in the volcano's quarries.

Several interpretations of their meaning have been put forward. The most probable is that the *moai* represent ancestors, chiefs, or other high-ranking individuals who held an important place in Easter Island's history; this theory relies in part on the observations of Cook, who noticed that the statues had names "to which they sometimes prefix the word Moi, and sometimes annex Areekee. The latter signifies Chief, and the former Burying or Sleeping-place." The statues of Rano Raraku and of the *ahu* had names that could be those of deified ancestors or sculptors. Some were derived from distinctive signs: the "Tattooed One" bears tattoos, "Twisted Neck" bows its head, and "Stinker" appears to be

L eft: *Moai* heads.

O pposite: A *moai* with a *pukao*.

B elow: The inner quarry of Rano Raraku. Alfred Métraux wrote: "The quarry is situated on the southwest slope and in the interior of the crater, where the tufa is most easily accessible…. Behind the swarms of statues standing on the grassy slope of the volcano is the army of those about to be born."

burdened with a bad smell. Other names relate to the place where the *moai* stand, and even to the birds that frequent the vicinity. As in Central Polynesia, the sacred nature of these anthropomorphic statues was temporary and depended on the rites that made the gods enter them.

Giants with Massive Bodies and Enormously Elongated Heads

The *moai* on the *ahu* are imposing and majestic. Their height generally varies from about eleven to eighteen feet. The most impressive of these statues is at the *ahu* Te Pito Te Kura on the north coast; it is about thirty-three feet high, and its weight is estimated to be ninety tons.

As time went on, the monumental statuary tended to take on gigantic proportions and simpler, standardized forms. The first *moai* may date from the 10th century, but most of them are attributed to the 14th and 15th centuries. However, statues different from the *moai* were already being set up on the *ahu* in the 8th century. Smaller sculptures in a different style have been given even earlier dates. They sometimes have aberrant forms and are carved in different materials, such as basalt or volcanic scoria; some could date back to the very earliest period of Easter Island's history.

"The bottom of the funnel [at Rano Kao] is occupied by a lake lined by rushes that serves as a watering place for livestock. Green slopes close off the horizon, making this pocket a world apart, enshrined in the island."
Pierre Loti
L'Ile de Pâques, 1872

Rano Kao, as seen in an 1878 lithograph.

The *Moai* Quarries Capture the Imagination of All Those Who Have Gazed on Them

The quarries of the stone giants are without doubt one of the most impressive places on the island. Close to the Poike peninsula, the open-air quarries are cut into the slopes of Rano Raraku volcano, extending up to about five hundred feet. This volcano was chosen for the quality of its rock, which offered excellent material for sculpture. The quarries were generally dug in places where the tuff was easily accessible. In the quarries, almost three hundred statues have been counted, but the sediments

On this islet of sixty-four square miles, nine hundred *moai* lie near the *ahu* and in the quarry of Rano Raraku. In the picture above the statues are still in their extraction cavities.

on the slopes have buried many others at the foot of the volcano. They were abandoned at different stages of manufacture: Some are barely roughed out, but others are finely worked and ready for transportation. Their average size varies from sixteen to twenty-three feet. The most impressive, "El Gigante," sixty-five feet in length, occupies the full extent of a ridge of the mountain. It would have weighed between 145 and 165 tons. No attempt was made to free this giant from its almost inaccessible place in the rock wall. No doubt it is just one of those gigantic petroglyphs, intended to stay as it was, like recumbent figures in Western cathedrals.

The kneeling statue Tukuturi, at the foot of Rano Raraku, is Polynesian in style.

The Giants Sleep Forever

Inside the crater, numerous cavities bear witness to the sculptors' relentless work. The wall was worked only in the places where the rock is of excellent quality.

The impression that emanates from this unusual site is that the sculptors have just stopped work on these enormous megaliths, leaving their tools on site. Hundreds of statues are in the process of being made. Some empty cavities bear the imprint of the colossus born from the volcano, while others are occupied by broken statues or by perfectly worked giants.

The hundreds of unfinished *moai* in these immense workshops have helped to reconstruct the different phases of manufacture.

The sculptors worked in a cramped space around the block, in channels that were about two feet wide and five feet deep. They carved the figures as if they were lying on their backs; the sculptors began with the head, then moved to the body and finally the sides. The polishing and the finishing touches were

The engraved back of a *moai* dug out by Katherine Routledge in 1914 (above).

The relatively soft block of scoria was attacked with stone picks. Several *moai* are still fixed to their sockets by a thin "keel" of rock (left).

completed before the statue was fully detached. This last operation was delicate, and statues were often damaged: The sculpture was undermined until it rested on nothing more than a kind of thin "keel," which was then pierced with holes. These cavities were then enlarged, and the keel was gradually replaced by chocks of stone. This arrangement enabled people to position logs or another device for moving the statues out of their extraction cavity; several statues are today lying on beds of small rocks that could have facilitated their transportation. Finally the statues were conveyed to the foot of the volcano, where they were set up temporarily by sliding them into a hole or onto a terrace made in the slope. Here the sculptor finished the *moai*'s back.

Tuu Ko Ihu Ordered the Statues to Walk to the Sanctuary

Once they were finished, the stone giants were transported to *ahu* that were sometimes more than twelve miles away. How the three hundred statues eventually set up on the sanctuaries were moved remains a mystery today. Oral traditions do not provide any satisfactory technical evidence. The Easter Islanders invoke the mythical chief Tuu Ko Ihu, the god Make Make, or even specialist priests who ordered the statues to "walk" and place themselves on their respective *ahu*. The lack of

"And who can tell the age of these gods?… Eaten by lichens, they seem to have the patina of countless centuries.… There are also some fallen ones and broken ones. Others, buried up to the nostrils by time and the rising soil level, seem to be sniffing the ground."

Pierre Loti
L'Ile de Pâques, 1872

information about this subject has unleashed people's imaginations, especially as the statues' weight has always been overestimated. There has been talk of three hundred, four hundred, and even five hundred tons. In actual fact, the tuff is a relatively light material: A sixteen-foot statue weighs a maximum of eighteen tons.

Nonetheless, it is true that the transportation of these giants, the heaviest of which is about eighty tons, was no mean feat, although the difficulties seem to lie not so much in moving them as in transporting them without damaging them. On Easter Island, the

The *ahu* Akivi (above), one of the largest on the island, is 1.25 miles from the west coast. The platform, extended by two lateral wings, is 260 feet long. The *ahu* is approached by a paved ramp.

Opposite: A *moai* that has fallen from an *ahu*.

problem was to imagine a lifting system requiring a minimum of wood, since the first European visitors had found only meager clusters of trees.

In fact, there was not always a shortage of timber. Recent research has proved that the island was originally wooded. Several species grew there, including the *Sophora toromiro* and a type of palm similar to *Jubaea chilensis*, the Chilean wine palm; this tree's wood was perfectly suited to the manufacture of levers, sledges, or rollers. The bark of a shrub, *Triumfetta*, was invaluable for the fabrication of solid ropes.

The Statues Brought to Life

Once the statue had reached the foot of the *ahu*, the finishing touches were completed, and then the *moai* was erected and placed on its pedestal.

Some *moai*, like those of the *ahu* Ko Te Riku wear on their heads an enormous cylinder of red volcanic tuff. This *pukao* overhangs the eyes like a visor. Topped with a conical knob, this headgear has been interpreted in various ways: basket, crown, hat, turban, diadem of flowers.... For Métraux, it was a hairstyle, a kind of topknot worn by lofty dignitaries at the time of the Europeans' arrival.

Finally, it is likely that numerous *moai* were painted once they were set up on their *ahu*. The statues of *ahu* Vinapu still bear traces of red color; the Orongo sculpture, now in the Museum of Mankind in London, was painted red and white. The statues came to life when they were given sight: Two sockets were carved to house an eye carved in white coral, a scarce commodity that was available only when it was washed up by the sea.

Most statues were toppled and broken during the tribal wars. Some of the few *moai* still standing at the beginning of the 19th century were knocked down by Western expeditions.

Left: A *moai* at *ahu* Nau Nau with its eyes restored.

In 1838 the French Admiral Abel Dupetit-Thouars Was the Last European To See Any Statues Standing

By 1864, when the missionaries settled on Easter Island, no statues remained upright. Cook, La Pérouse, and others were struck by the numerous *moai* that lay on the ground. The islanders' traditions attribute the toppling of the statues to the wars that ravaged the island at the end of the 18th century or the beginning of the 19th. As in other parts of Polynesia, the victors humiliated the vanquished by destroying their social and ancestral sanctuaries.

In 1872 the sailors of the French frigate *La Flore* took on board a colossal head that is now in the Musée de l'Homme in Paris. One of the heads belonged to the figure on page 97.

Page 96: Rano Raraku seen from *ahu* Tonga Riki.

DOCUMENTS

Seafarers and missionaries, archaeologists
and ethnologists, writers and tourists:
What are all these Westerners looking for on
the most isolated island in the Great Ocean?

The Seafarers' View

*Few European seafarers
ventured into the waters near
Easter Island, one of the
remotest islands in the world.
But this mysterious and desolate
land, with its strange stone
statues, struck all those who
visited it. They left us vivid and
detailed accounts.*

Fifty years after Roggeveen, James Cook
reached the Pacific Islands (opposite).
Below: Easter Island in an 1878 engraving.

*Jacob Roggeveen kept a journal during his
voyage of 1721–2, when he became the first
Westerner to land on Easter Island.*

They had seen very distinctly ahead
to starboard a low flat island.… We gave
to…the land the name of the Paasch
Eyland [Easter Island], because it was
discovered and found by us on Easter
Day.…

In the morning Captain Bouman…
brought to our ship a Paaschlander with
his vessel who was quite naked, without
having the least covering in front of
what modesty forbids being named
more clearly. This poor person appeared
to be very glad to see us, and marvelled
greatly at the construction of our
ship.… After we had amused ourselves
enough with him, and he with us, we
sent him back to shore in his canoe,
having been presented with two blue
strings of beads round his neck, a small
mirror, a pair of scissors, and other such
trifles, in which he seemed to take
special pleasure and satisfaction.…

Very many canoes came to the ships.
These people showed at this time their
great eagerness for all that they saw
and were so bold that they took the
hats and caps of the sailors from their
heads and jumped with their plunder
overboard, for they are extremely good
swimmers, as was shown by the fact
that a large number came swimming
from land to the ships.…

We set out in the morning with
three boats and two sloops, manned
with 134 men, and all armed with a
musket, cartridge pouch and sword…
we marched forward a little…to our
great astonishment and without any
expectation it was heard that four to five
musket-shots from behind us were
made…more than thirty muskets

were let off, and the Indians being completely surprised and frightened by this fled, leaving behind 10 to 12 dead, besides the wounded.... The Under Mate...came to me saying that...one of the inhabitants grasped the muzzle of his musket in order to take it from him by force, whom he pushed back; then that another Indian tried to pull the coat of a sailor off his body, and that some of the inhabitants, seeing our resistance, picked up stones with a menacing gesture of throwing at us, by which by all appearance the shooting by my small troop had been caused....

After lapse of a little time they brought a large quantity of sugar-cane, fowls, yams and bananas; but we gave them to understand by signs that we wanted nothing except only the fowls, being about 60 in number, and 30 bunches of bananas, for which we paid them the value amply with striped linen, with which they appeared to be well pleased and satisfied....

The ears of these people from youth are...stretched in the lobes and the innermost part cut out.... Now when these Indians have to do something,

and these ear-pendants through swinging hither and thither would be troublesome to them, they take them off and pull the opening of the lobe up over the edge of the ear, which makes a strange laughable appearance.... These people have snow-white teeth, and are outstandingly strong in the teeth....

Concerning the religion of these people, of this we could get no full knowledge because of the shortness of our stay; we merely observed that they set fires before some particularly high erected stone images, and then sitting down on their heels with bowed heads, they bring the palms of their hands together, moving them up and down. These stone images at first caused us to be struck with astonishment, because we could not comprehend how it was possible that these people, who are devoid of heavy thick timber for making any machines, as well as strong ropes, nevertheless had been able to erect such images, which were fully 30 feet high and thick in proportion.

The Journal of Jacob Roggeveen,
Translated and edited by
Andrew Sharp, 1970

A humanist philosophy, a rationalist optimism, and a faith in the progress of the Age of Enlightenment shine throughout the account of the voyage made by Jean-François de Galaup, Comte de La Pérouse (above).

On the 4th of April, when I was at no more than sixty leagues distance from Easter Island, I saw no birds, and the wind was at north-north-west. It is probable that if I had not known the position of the island to a certainty, I should have thought that I had passed it, and should have put about. I made these reflections on the spot, and cannot help confessing that the discovery of islands is only due to chance, and that very often the most sagacious calculations have only served to put navigators out of their way....

At day break, I steered for Cook's Bay, which of all those in the island is the best sheltered from easterly winds. It is consequently only open to the west; and the weather was so fine, that I was in

hopes it would not blow from that quarter for several days. At eleven o'clock I was only a league from the anchorage. The *Astrolabe* had already let go her anchor, and I dropped mine very near her; but the bottom shelved so suddenly that neither of them held, and we were obliged to heave them up and make two boards in order to regain the anchorage.

This accident did not damp the ardour of the Indians. They swam after us till we were a league in the offing, and came on board with a smiling look and an air of security which gave me a high opinion of their disposition. Men, more suspicious than they, would have been afraid, when we got under way again, of being carried away from their native land. But the idea of such an act of perfidy never seemed to present itself to their mind. They were in the midst of us naked and without arms, having only a bit of pack-thread tied around their loins to confine a bundle of grass which concealed their private parts....

At day break I made every preparation for our landing. I had reason to flatter myself I should find friends on shore, since I had loaded all those with presents who had come from thence over night; but from the accounts of other navigators, I was well aware, that these Indians are only children of a larger growth, in whose eyes our different commodities appear so desirable as to induce them to put every means in practice to get possession of them. I thought it necessary, therefore, to restrain them by fear, and ordered our landing to be made with a little military parade; accordingly it was effected with four boats and twelve armed soldiers. M. de Langle and myself were followed by all the passengers and officers, except those who were wanted on board to carry on the duty of the two frigates; so that we amounted to about seventy persons, including our boats' crews.

Four or five hundred Indians were waiting for us on the shore; they were unarmed; some of them cloathed in pieces of white or yellow stuff, but the greater number naked: many were tattooed, and had their faces painted red; their shouts and countenances were expressive of joy; and they came forward to offer us their hands, and to facilitate our landing.…

As man by habit accustoms himself to almost any situation, these people appeared less miserable to me than to Captain Cook and Mr. Forster. They arrived here after a long and disagreeable voyage; in want of every thing, and sick of the scurvy; they found neither water, wood, nor hogs; a few fowls, bananas, and potatoes are but feeble resources in these circumstances. Their narratives bear testimony to their situation. Ours was infinitely better: the crews enjoyed the most perfect health; we had taken in at Chile every thing that was necessary for many months, and we only desired of these people the privilege of doing them good: we brought them goats, sheep, and hogs; we had seeds of orange, lemon, and cotton trees, of maize, and, in short, of every species of plants, which was likely to flourish in the island.…

On the Raising of the Statues

No more remains, but to explain how it was possible to raise, without engines, so very considerable a weight; but as it is certainly a very light volcanic stone, it would be easy, with levers five or six toises [thirty or forty feet] long, and by slipping stones underneath, as Captain Cook very well explains it, to lift a much more considerable weight; a hundred men would be sufficient for this purpose, for indeed there would not have been room for more. Thus the wonder disappears; we restore to nature her stone of Lapillo, which is not factitious; and have reason to think, that if there are no monuments of modern construction in the island, it is because all ranks in it are become equal, and that a man has but little temptation to make himself king of a people almost naked, and who live on potatoes and yams; and on the other hand, these Indians not being able to go to war from the want of neighbours, have no need of a chief.…

On the Mores of the Easter Islanders

It is certain, that these people have not the same ideas of theft that we have; with them, probably no shame is attached to it; but they very well knew, that they committed an unjust action, since they immediately took to flight, in order to avoid the punishment which they doubtless feared, and which we should certainly have inflicted on them in proportion to the crime, had we made any considerable stay in the island; for our extreme lenity might have ended by producing disagreeable consequences.

No one, after having read the narratives of the later navigators, can take the Indians of the South Sea for savages; they have on the contrary made very great progress in civilization, and I think them as corrupt as the circumstances in which they are placed will allow them to be. This opinion of them is not founded upon the different thefts which they committed, but upon the manner in which they effected them. The most hardened rogues of Europe are not such great hypocrites as these islanders; all their caresses were feigned; their countenances never expressed a single sentiment of truth; and the man of whom it was necessary to be most distrustful, was the Indian to whom a present had that moment been made, and who appeared the most eager to return for it a thousand little services.

They brought to us by force young girls of thirteen or fourteen years of age, in the hope of receiving pay for them; the repugnance of those young females was a proof, that in this respect the custom of the country was violated. Not a single Frenchman made use of the barbarous right which was given him; and if there were some moments dedicated to nature, the desire and consent were mutual, and the women made the first advances....

The exactness with which they measured the ship showed, that they had not been inattentive spectators of our arts; they examined our cables, anchors, compass, and wheel, and they returned the next day with a cord to take the measure over again, which made me think, that they had had some discussions on shore upon the subject, and that they had still doubts relative to it. I esteem them far less, because they appeared to me capable of reflection. One reflection will, perhaps, escape them, namely, that we employed no violence against them; though they were not ignorant of our being armed, since the mere presenting a firelock in sport made them run away: on the contrary, we landed on the island only with an intention to do them service; we heaped presents upon them, we caressed the children; we sowed in their fields all kinds of useful seeds; presented them with hogs, goats, and sheep, which probably will multiply; we demanded nothing in return: nevertheless they

T*he "Blossom" off Sandwich Bay*, watercolor by William Henry Smyth.

threw stones at us, and robbed us of every thing which it was possible for them to take away. It would, perhaps, have been imprudent in other circumstances to conduct ourselves with so much lenity; but I had resolved to go away in the evening, and I flattered myself that at day break, when they no longer perceived our ships, they would attribute our speedy departure to the just displeasure we entertained at their proceedings, and that this reflection might amend them; though this idea is a little chimerical, it is of no great consequence to navigators, as the island offers scarcely any resource to ships that may touch there, besides being at no great distance from the Society Isles.

Jean-François de Galaup,
Comte de La Pérouse,
*A Voyage Round the World in the Years
1785–1788*, Vols. I and II, 1798

Born in 1793, the French admiral Abel Dupetit-Thouars (above) stopped at Easter Island in 1838 before establishing the French protectorate on Tahiti in 1842.

We had scarcely left the eastern point of the island when, in front of the Spanish bay, we met five canoes heading toward us; they were each occupied by two men, and three of these canoes also contained a woman, sitting right at the front, squatting, or lying on her stomach to form less of an obstacle while sailing or, perhaps too, to give the canoe more stability.

When the frigate stopped to make some observations, these natives unhesitatingly climbed on board; they seemed to be used to visits of this kind; they danced and performed a thousand antics that greatly amused us; they were very gay and displayed a quite extraordinary liveliness in both movements and mind. However, if I had not had strong reason since then to believe in their bravery, I might have thought that, being intimidated by a large crew, which no doubt they were not expecting to encounter, they were trying to forget their position. Nevertheless, if they felt any fear, it was cleverly concealed and even more promptly dispelled; they put on a bold front. Using sign language, the men asked to be shaved, and this was granted. One of them then received a cap and collar as presents and immediately put them on. He proudly walked about the deck, admiring himself as if he were richly dressed. All the natives frequently and actively repeated the word *miro*, and grew impatient when it was not understood at all: This is the name of the wood used by the Polynesians to make their canoes. This object was what they desired most keenly, and they used several methods to make themselves understood; they did not want to eat or drink; they seemed to have a poor opinion of knives and scissors; fishhooks gave them great pleasure, as did mirrors and colored handkerchiefs.

While the crew was busy gathering in the laundered washing, one of these savages displayed very great skill at theft; he sat, as if unaware of the fact, on a red tie and hid it very skillfully in a little plaited bag he had with him; when he was made to give it back, he showed no bad temper nor any surprise at being discovered, and immediately recommenced the same trick, hoping to be more successful this time.

For a while, the canoes—which had not been able to follow the frigate when it moved away a little—stayed some distance behind; as soon as one of the women noticed, she began to cry out loud and wail pitifully, like a child: She was immediately imitated by several of the other savages, but they were all quickly reassured on seeing the frigate stop again. (This apprehension on the part of the savages, this fear of being carried off, was not without cause: several of the whaling ships that lacked men had taken some on various Polynesian islands, and did not always bring them back to their homes when fishing was finished.) When we had completed our observations, we had to leave: All the natives, men and women, jumped into the water and swam back to their canoes....

The men were tattooed, and so were the women around the mouth, on the forehead, around the hairline, and on the front of the thighs so that it looked as though they were wearing a blue apron. The most striking aspect of the behavior of these women was their appearance of modesty: No doubt they were not ashamed of their nudity, but in their posture there was a kind of visible embarrassment that was certainly a natural effect of modesty: They felt a kind of shame at appearing thus before us, and appeared to ask our forgiveness for their slovenliness. The embarrassment they displayed at being naked is also a sure proof of progress and in some way a step forward toward civilization; for it is well known that the savages who saw clothed men for the first time never thought of drawing a parallel to their disadvantage, they merely regarded them with the curious amusement that we feel on seeing dogs and monkeys dressed up, and some even carried their curiosity so far as to check whether the clothes were attached to the skin, like feathers to birds. When we encouraged our companions to dance, they needed little persuasion, and performed a very entertaining hopping dance in front of us. This dance, like those of all savage peoples, represented the most important drama in life.

After this first visit, we were sailing westward with great speed when we heard shouts coming from the open sea; soon we perceived two men swimming toward us and uttering cries that could be heard from a very great distance; they each seemed to be on a piece of broken canoe, of which only the prow was visible; I sent a rowing boat to fetch them: owing to their great distance from land, I feared they might become victims of the curiosity we had aroused; because I supposed that their canoe had in fact broken up. But we were very surprised to find that these natives were each sitting astride a bundle of rushes, shaped like a sheaf of corn; to be sure of a more favorable reception, they brought bananas, sweet potatoes, and

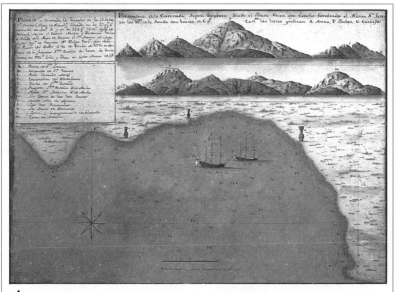

An 18th-century map depicting the giant stone statues of Easter Island.

yams, enclosed in their reeds. They urged us to go ashore where we would find many women and provisions; to make themselves understood they used a very meaningful pantomime, which made things very clear. They again gave us cause to notice the ease with which they remembered and pronounced the words they heard; but, like our first visitors, their minds never remained focused on any object for more than a second, with the notable exception of wood, which they all asked for with equal eagerness and the same entreaties.

We had great difficulty in getting rid of our new visitors; they laughed at our threats and no longer wanted to leave us; however, they decided to go when I gave the order for their reed bundles to be thrown in the sea; they immediately dashed after them

and returned to the island....

Easter Island is not visited often: it is not on any vessel's route. When coming from Mexico, it is only rarely that winds are in opposition for so long as to force a ship to sail west as far as its meridian, and the whaling ships or other vessels that sail the Pacific Ocean have no interest in going there since they will find no water or wood; the provisions it produces are very scarce, and quite apart from the difficulty one would have, no doubt, in procuring even a small quantity, they are not very suitable as supplies at sea.

Abel Dupetit-Thouars,
Voyage Autour du Monde sur la Frégate la Vénus, Pendant les Années 1836–1839
(A Voyage Around the World in the Frigate *La Vénus* During the Years 1836–1839), 1840

Loti's Island

On 3 January 1872 the frigate La Flore *anchored off Easter Island; on board was Julien Viaud, alias Pierre Loti. "As an aspiring naval cadet, I wrote down my day-to-day impressions in my notebooks."*

A bove: Pierre Loti. Opposite: The crew of *La Flore* at Valparaíso in 1871.

3 January 1872

A few days ago, to reach here, we left those routes that are usually followed by ships across the Pacific, because Easter Island is on nobody's route. It was discovered by chance, and the few seafarers who visited it every now and then have left contradictory accounts. The population, whose origins are surrounded by a troubling mystery, is gradually dying out for unknown reasons; we have been told that only a few dozen savages remain, starving and fearful and feeding on roots; in the middle of the loneliness of the sea, it too will soon be no more than a solitary place whose giant statues will remain its only guardians. There is nothing there, not even a supply of fresh water; and moreover the breakers and reefs prevent one from landing there most of the time.

As for us, we are going to explore it and, if possible, take one of the ancient stone statues, which our admiral would like to bring back to France.

The strange island approaches slowly and takes shape; beneath the overcast sky, it displays reddish craters and gloomy rocks. A strong wind blows, and the sea is covered with white foam.

Rapa Nui is the name given to Easter Island by the natives—and in the mere sound of this word, it seems to me, there is sadness, savagery and darkness.... The mists of time, the murky origins, or the darkness of the sky, one cannot really say what kind of obscurity it is; but it is certain that these black clouds, which envelop the land as it appears before us, correspond well to my imagination....

At midday the expedition is ready to go and look for the great idol. In the frigate's launch we loaded enormous hoisting gear, a kind of improvised

wagon and a fatigue party of a hundred men, led by a lieutenant….

The natives have gathered en masse on the beach and utter piercing cries to receive us. Since yesterday the news of the impending removal of the statue has spread among them, and they have rushed over from all parts of the island to watch us at work; even some of those who live at La Pérouse Bay, on the other side of the island, have come; we also see many new faces.

The lieutenant commanding the fatigue party insists that the hundred men should make their way to the *maraï* in ranks and in step, with bugles sounding the march; the populace is sent into a state of indescribable joy by music it had never heard before, and it becomes difficult to keep the sailors in good order, with all these beautiful half-naked girls gamboling and playing around them.

At the *maraï*, for example, no further discipline is possible; it becomes a crazy confusion of naval tunics and tattooed flesh, a frenzy of movement and uproar; everybody is touching each other, crowding together, singing, shouting and dancing. After an hour, with blows from crowbars and levers, everything is knocked about, and the statues more overturned and broken than ever, but we still do not know which one will be chosen.

One of them, which seems less heavy and less worn, is lying head down, with its nose in the earth; its face is not yet known, and we shall have to turn it over to see. It yields to the efforts of the levers manipulated with great shouts; it pivots around on itself and falls on to its back with a dull thud. Now that it has been turned over and it has fallen, more furious dancing takes place and a louder clamor goes up. Twenty savages jump on its stomach and gambol there like madmen…. The ancient dead of the primitive races have never heard such a racket since they began their sleep under their mounds—except perhaps for when these statues lost their balance, all shaken together by some earthquake, or perhaps falling from old age, one by one, face down in the grass.

It is definitely this one, the last one to

A fan given by Pierre Loti to Louise Barthou, showing statues on Easter Island.

be touched and turned over, that we are going to take away; not the whole body, but only its head, its big head that already weighs four or five tons; so we set about sawing through its neck. Fortunately it is made of a fairly crumbly kind of volcanic stone, and the saws bite well, though they squeak terribly....

At the very end of sunset, I return to sit with my five friends facing the sea, at the point where we have already adopted the habit of waiting together for the arrival of the rowing boats. This will perhaps be the last time, for I see over there, in the distance, the launch returning to the frigate and, in the middle of the crowd of sailors dressed in white, the great brown head of the idol which is departing in their company; therefore the exercise has succeeded to perfection, and we have the chance to leave tomorrow. I would almost say "too bad," because I would willingly have stayed longer.

But in the evening, as I am about to lie down in my hammock, I am called to the commanding officer, and I have a feeling that something new is afoot for the next day.

He does indeed inform me that our departure has been postponed for twenty-four hours. Tomorrow he intends to go with several officers to the remotest part of the island where some idols, very different from those we know, are still standing.... And he asks me if I would like to accompany him. Needless to say, I am dying to do so. But tomorrow I am on duty, alas!, having spent the whole of today walking around. "I'll square things with the admiral," he says, adding with a laugh, "On one condition…" Ah yes, the drawings! I shall have to draw the statues from all sides and for everyone. … As much as you like, as long as you take me along!

Pierre Loti, *L'Ile de Pâques, Journal d'Un Aspirant de la Flore*, (Easter Island, Journal of a Young Aspiring Naval Cadet on *La Flore*), 1988

An Islander "Reads" a *Kohau Rongo Rongo* Tablet

A man called Ure Vaeiko, one of the patriarchs of the island, professes to have been under instructions in the art of the hieroglyphic reading at the time of the Peruvian visit, and claims to understand most of the characters. Negotiations were opened with him for a translation of the two tablets purchased; but he declined to furnish any information on the ground that it had been forbidden by the priests. Presents of money and valuables were sent to him from time to time, but he invariably replied to all overtures that he was now old and feeble and had but a short time to live, and declined most positively to ruin his chances for salvation by doing what his Christian instructors had forbidden. Finally the old fellow, to avoid temptation, took to the hills with the determination to remain in hiding until after the departure of the *Mohican*. It was a matter of the utmost importance that the subject should be thoroughly investigated before leaving the island, and unscrupulous strategy was the only resource after fair means had failed....

In a heavy down-pour of rain we crossed the island from Vinapu to Mataveri with Mr. Salmon, and found, as had been expected, that old Ure Vaeiko had sought the shelter of his own home on this rough night. He was asleep when we entered and took charge of the establishment. When he found escape impossible he became sullen, and refused to look at or touch a tablet. As a compromise it was proposed that he should relate some of the ancient traditions. This was readily acceded to, because the opportunity of relating the legends to an interested audience did not often occur, and the positive pleasure to be derived from such an occasion could not be neglected. During the recital certain stimulants that had been provided for such an emergency were produced, and though not pressed upon our ancient friend, were kept prominently before him until, as the night grew old and the narrator weary, he was included as the "cup that cheers" made its occasional rounds. A judicious indulgence in present comforts dispelled all fears in regard to the future state, and at an auspicious moment the

photographs of the tablets owned by the bishop were produced for inspection. Old Ure Vaeiko had never seen a photograph before, and was surprised to find how faithfully they reproduced the tablets which he had known in his young days. A tablet would have met with opposition, but no objection could be urged against a photograph, especially something possessed by the good bishop, whom he had been instructed to reverence. The photographs were recognized immediately and the appropriate legend related with fluency and without hesitation from beginning to end....

Ure Vaeiko's fluent interpretation of the tablet was not interrupted, though it became evident that he was not actually reading the characters. It was noticed that the shifting of position did not accord with the number of symbols on the lines, and afterwards when the photograph of another tablet was substituted, the same story was continued without the change being discovered. The old fellow was quite discomposed when charged with fraud at the close of an all-night session, and at first maintained that the characters were all understood, but he could not give the significance of hieroglyphics copied indiscriminately from tablets already marked. He explained at great length that the actual value and significance of the symbols had been forgotten, but the tablets were recognized by unmistakable features and the interpretation of them was beyond question; just as a person might recognize a book in a foreign language and be perfectly sure of the contents without being able to actually read it.

William Thomson
Te Pito Te Henua, or Easter Island, 1891

The Missionaries

In 1864, moved by the sufferings endured by the islanders, Brother Eugène Eyraud disembarked on Easter Island. Soon other missionaries would join him. The news that they regularly sent to their superiors gives a valuable account of the daily life of the indigenous population.

Brother Eugène Eyraud Was the First Foreign Person to Take an Interest in the Statuettes and the *Kohau Rongo Rongo* Tablets

Valparaíso, December 1864

No doubt you wanted many details about our islanders' religion. As far as I have been able to ascertain during the nine months of my stay, religion seems to occupy quite a minimal place in their life. My knowledge of their language is too imperfect, it is true, to enable me to pose many questions about this subject. But, although I have always lived with them in the greatest familiarity, I have never been able to come upon any positive act linked to a religious cult. In all the houses many statuettes are seen, about a foot high, representing male figures, fishes, birds, etc. They are undoubtedly idols, but I have not noticed that they have been attributed any kinds of honors. I have occasionally seen the natives taking these statuettes,

lifting them into the air, making some gestures, and accompanying all of it with a sort of dance and an insignificant song. What do they mean by that? I believe they do not know much about it. They do quite simply what they have seen their fathers do, without offering it any further thought. If you ask them what it means, they answer you, as they do about their games, that such is the custom of the country.

Nor have I seen any religious rites when someone dies. When someone is ill, the whole treatment consists of taking them outside the house during the day, and putting them back inside at night. If the sick person breathes his last, he is wrapped in a straw mat a little longer than the corpse, the mat is tied with "purau" cord, and then the whole thing is taken and placed on the shore, opposite the house; these bodies wrapped in their mats are placed on a heap of stones, or on a kind of wooden trestle, with their heads toward the sea. As the whole population is spread around the island, dried corpses covered with mats are encountered all along the coast, though people seem to pay them little attention. I do not know what sort of idea these poor savages have of death or the other life....

In all their houses tablets of wood or sticks covered with many kinds of hieroglyphic signs can be found: figures of animals unknown on the island, which the natives trace by means of sharp stones. What significance do they attach to these characters? They probably know very little about them. Each figure no doubt has its own name; but the little they make of these tablets

A village at Cook's Bay on Easter Island in the late 19th century.

makes me inclined to think that these signs, the remains of a primitive script, now represent for them only a custom that they preserve without searching for the meaning.

The natives know how neither to read nor write. However, they count very easily, and have words to represent all the numbers. They even have a measure of time; it is a lunar year. But here too their memories are growing weak, and they do not agree on the number of moons. One thing that is quite noteworthy: These savages display an extreme interest in everything connected with these questions. When I spoke of the months, the sunrise, etc., everybody drew near: Everyone, including the old people, came to take their place among the pupils.

Brother Eugène Eyraud
Letter to the Very Reverend Father
Superior General

Father Gaspard Zumbohm Arrives in Triumph on Easter Island

October 1879

Five months had already passed since that good Brother Eugène, the true founder of the Rapa Nui mission, disembarked on this island with Father Hippolyte, when I was sent there, together with Brother Théodule, by our Provincial, who at that time was Father Olivier.

We were transported on the *Tampico* commanded by Captain Dutrou-Bornier. When the ship drew near the coast, almost all the inhabitants came to meet us in Hanga Roa Bay. The clothing of these Indians was at the time extremely primitive: I shall try to describe it for you.

First of all everybody—men and

women, but not children—wore a belt; besides, all the women and most of the men were decked out in a kind of fabric, in the form of a long square, which they threw around their shoulders and attached at the neck by a knot or a string; they then brought together the edges of this piece, holding them in their hands, and thus wrapped themselves up as they pleased and according to the length of the piece. This length varied greatly, depending on each one's wealth: The chiefs had capes that extended as far as the knees....

Among our visitors we noticed a young boy who seemed to be about fourteen; he was well dressed and wore a kepi on his head. We were told this was the young king; he alone of all the natives had been baptized. We also made out three figures in the crowd whose appearance contrasted with that of the other islanders; they seemed to be very busy keeping order: These were three good Christians from Mangareva (one of the Gambier Islands) who, out of devotion, had accompanied Father Hippolyte and Brother Eugène on this arduous mission; they made themselves very useful, either as interpreters or in setting a good example and directing work.

As soon as we had arrived, two Indians came and offered to carry us to the beach on their backs. We accepted this service, which was then rewarded with garments. I shall never be able to convey my feelings during this journey: the kindness, the joy, and the pride with which my porter carried out his job filled my soul with sweet hope. Once I had my feet on land, I found myself surrounded by such a dense crowd that I could scarcely move forward. From all

sides I was asked questions to which I was unable to reply, since I did not yet understand the language of this land; however, I understood the kind greetings of these good people, because their tone and their gestures conveyed more than their words. I was longing to get away from these demonstrations, which I found excessively moving: So I was happy to enter the mission chapel, to give thanks and enjoy a little calm and repose, after embracing my colleagues with a joy that I need not describe to you.

But we had to think about unloading our effects: The Oceanians found a new joy in helping us with this operation: The sight of various objects with which they were completely unfamiliar caused them some mirth; and when the wheelbarrow was loaded up and began to move, our islanders gave shouts of admiration: The turning wheel seemed like a living being to them.

We had brought a cow and its calf; when these two animals headed for our enclosure, the astonishment was greater than ever. But the greatest enthusiasm was shown when one of the sailors landed with the fine horse on which he was mounted—at this moment there was even a kind of panic for, imagining that the rider and his steed were a single entity, our good people began to tremble; we saw some who ran away as fast as their legs could carry them; others lay on the ground; those who were courageous enough to take a closer look at the phenomenon were absolutely astounded to see the animal split up, that is, the man got down from his mount. When disembarkation was over, a signal was sounded: It was the call to prayers. At the same moment, the chapel opened and all the islanders ran there. The most learned were in front, the others stayed at the back, and many even had to remain outside because the building was too small. Once everyone was gathered together like this, Father Hippolyte made the sign of the cross and said in a loud voice: "*I te igoa note Matua,*" etc., that is, "In the name of the Father…".

Everybody followed and sang reverently: It was truly an admirable and highly edifying spectacle. To think that in so short a time a good number of these savages had already learned the main prayers; they knew the first elements of the catechism and were starting to understand the explanations with which one tried to place the great truths of our holy religion within their grasp.

Father Gaspard Zumbohm,
Letter to the director of the Annales
de la Congrégation des Sacrés-Coeurs
de Jésus et de Marie

Years After the Missionaries Had Withdrawn, Katherine Routledge Investigated the Islanders' Original Religion

The remarks of the missionaries on native customs, particularly those dealing with their ceremonies, reflect credit on the observers at a time when such things were too often thought beneath notice.… Their ethnological work was, however, limited by more pressing exigencies, by the difficulties of locomotion on the island, and by the language.… It is a curious fact that so completely were the terraces now ruined that the Fathers never allude to the statues, and seem scarcely to have realized their existence; but it is through them that we first hear of the wooden tablets carved with figures. The body

of professors acquainted with this art of writing perished, either in Peru or by epidemic, and this, in connection with the introduction of Christianity, led to great destruction of the existing specimens of this most interesting script. The natives said that they burnt the tablets in compliance with the orders of the missionaries, though such suggestion would hardly be needed in a country where wood is scarce; the Fathers, on the contrary, state that it was due to them that any were preserved. Some certainly were saved by their means and through the interest shown in them by Bishop Jaussen of Tahiti, while two or three found their way to museums after the natives became aware of their value; but some or all of these existing tablets are merely fragments of the original. The natives told us that an expert living on the south coast, whose house had been full of such glyphs, abandoned them at the call of the missionaries, on which a man named Niari, being of a practical mind, got hold of the discarded tablets and made a boat of them wherein he caught much fish.…

The other source of information which was open to us was the memory of the old people. If but little was known of the great works, it was possible that there might still linger knowledge of customs or folk-lore which would throw indirect light on origins. This field proved to be astonishingly large, but it was even more difficult to collect facts from brains than out of stones. On our arrival there were still a few old people who were sufficiently grown up in the sixties to recall something of the old life; with the great majority of these, about a dozen in number, we gradually got in touch…it was a matter of anxious consideration whose testimony should first be recorded for fear that, meanwhile, others should be gathered to their fathers, and their store of knowledge lost for ever. Against the longer collection of extreme old age had to be put the fact that the memories of those a little younger were generally more clear and accurate. The feeling of responsibility from a scientific point of view was very great. Ten years ago more could have been done; ten years hence little or nothing will remain of this source of knowledge.…

Unfortunately, some of the old men who knew most were confined to the leper settlement some three miles north of Hanga Roa.… But how could one allow the last vestige of knowledge in Easter Island to die out without an effort? So I went, disinfected my clothes on return, studied, must it be confessed, my fingers and toes, and hoped for the best.

It would not be easy for a foreigner to reconstruct English society fifty years ago, even from the descriptions of well-educated old men; it is particularly difficult to arrive at the truth from the untutored mind. Even when the natives knew well what they were talking about, they would forget to mention some part of the story, which to them was self-evident, but at which the humble European could not be expected to guess. The bird story, for example, had for many months been wrestled with before it transpired precisely what was meant by the "first egg." Deliberate invention was rare, but, when memory was a little vague, there was a constant tendency to glide from what was remembered to what was imagined.…

The religion of the Islanders, employing the word in our sense, seems always to have been somewhat hazy, and the difficulty in grasping it now is increased by the fact that since becoming Roman Catholics they dislike giving the name of *atua*, or god, to their old deities; it only drops out occasionally. They term them *aku-aku*, which means spirits, or more frequently *tatane*, a word of which the derivation is obvious. The confusion of ideas was crystallized by a native, who gravely remarked that they were uncertain whether one of these beings was God or the Devil, so they "wrote to Tahiti, and Tahiti wrote to Rome, and Rome said he was not the Devil, he was God"; a modern view being apparently taken at headquarters of the evolution of religious ideas. Both these words, *tatane* and *aku-aku*, will be employed for supernatural beings, without prejudice to their original character, or claims to divinity; some of them were certainly the spirits of the dead, but had probably become deified; the ancestors of Hotu Matua were reported to have come with him to the island. They existed in large numbers, being both male and female, and were connected with different parts of the island; a list of about ninety was given, with their places of residence. No worship was paid, and the only notice taken of these supernatural persons was to mention before meals the names of those to whom a man owed special duty, and invite them to partake; it was etiquette to mention with your own the patron of any guest who was present. There was no sacrifice; the invitation to the supernatural power was purely formal, or restricted to the essence of the food only. Nevertheless, the *aku-aku*, in this at least being human, were amiable or the reverse according to whether or not they were well fed. If they were hungry, they ate women and children; if, on the contrary, they were well-disposed to a man, they would do work for him, and he would wake in the morning to find his potato-field dug....

There were no priests, but certain men, known as *koromaké*, practised spells which would secure the death of an enemy, and there was also the class known as *ivi-atua*, which included both men and women. The most important of these *ivi-atua*, of whom it was said there might be perhaps ten in the island, held commune with the *aku-aku*, others were able to prophesy, and could foresee the whereabouts of

fish or turtle, while some had the gift of seeing hidden things, and would demand contributions from a secreted store of bananas or potatoes, in a way which was very disconcerting to the owner....

On the border-line, between religion and magic, wherever, if anywhere, that line exists, was the position of the clan known as the Miru. Members of this group had, in the opinion of the islanders, the supernatural and valuable gift of being able to increase all food supplies, especially that of chickens, and this power was particularly in evidence after death. It has been known that certain skulls from Easter are marked with designs, such as the outline of a fish; these are crania of the Miru, and called *puoko-*

A photograph of Easter Islanders taken by Alfred Métraux during his 1934 expedition.

moa or fowl-heads, because they had, in particular, the quality of making hens lay eggs....

Investigating the *Moai* Quarry

Rano Raraku is…a volcanic cone containing a crater lake.…The mountain is composed of volcanic ash, which has been found in certain places to be particularly suitable for quarrying; it has been worked on the southern exterior slope, and also inside the crater both on the south and south-eastern sides. With perhaps a dozen exceptions, the whole of the images in the island have been made from it, and they have been dragged from this point up hill and down dale to adorn the terraces round the coast-line of the island.… [The stone is] a reddish brown colour.… It is composite in character, and embedded in the ash are numerous lapilli of metamorphic rock. Owing to the nature of this rock the earliest European visitors came to the conclusion that the material was factitious and that the statues were built of clay and stones.…

It remains to account for the vast number of images to be found in the quarry. A certain number have, no doubt, been abandoned prior to the general cessation of the work; in some cases a flaw has been found in the rock and the original plan has had to be given up.… But when all these instances have been subtracted, the amount of figures remaining in the quarries is still startlingly large when compared with the number which have been taken out of it.… Legendary lore throws no light on these matters, nor on the reasons which led to the desertion of this labyrinth of work; it has invented a story which entirely satisfies the native

mind and is repeated on every occasion. There was a certain old woman who lived at the southern corner of the mountain and filled the position of cook to the image-makers. She was the most important person of the establishment, and moved the images by supernatural power (*mana*), ordering them about at her will. One day, when she was away, the workers obtained a fine lobster, which had been caught on the west coast, and ate it up, leaving none for her; unfortunately they forgot to conceal the remains, and when the cook returned and found how she had been treated, she arose in her wrath, told all the images to fall down, and thus brought the work to a standstill.…

Descending from the quarries, we turn to the figures below.… On the slopes there are a few horizontal statues, but the great majority, both inside the crater and without, are still erect.… All stood with their backs to the mountain.… Every statue is buried in greater or less[er] degree, but while some are exposed as far as the elbow, in others only a portion of the top of the head can be seen above the surface, others no doubt are covered entirely.…

The questions which arise are obvious; do these buried statues differ in any way from those in the workings above, from those on the *ahu* or from one another? Were they put up on any foundation?… In the hope of throwing some light on these problems we started to dig them out. It had originally been thought that the excavation of one or two would give all the information which it was possible to obtain, but each case was found to have unique and instructive features, and we finally unearthed in this way, wholly or in part, some twenty or thirty statues....

Indications were found of two different methods of erection, and the mode may have been determined by the nature of the ground. By the first procedure the statue seems to have been placed on its face in the desired spot, and a hole to have been dug beneath the base. The other method was to undermine the base, with the statue lying face uppermost; in several instances a number of large stones were found behind the back of the figure, evidently having been used to wedge it while it was dragged to the vertical....

As Raraku is approached, a number of figures lie by the side of the modern track, others are round the base of the mountain, and yet other isolated specimens are scattered about the island. All these images are prostrate and lie on the surface of the ground, some on their backs and some on their faces. These were the ones which, according to legend, were being moved from the quarries to the *ahu* by the old lady when she stopped the work in her wrath....

There must, we felt, have been roads along which they were taken...looking towards the sea, along the level plain of the south coast, the old track was clearly seen; it was slightly raised over lower ground and depressed somewhat though higher, and along it every few hundred yards lay a statue.... [The road] was about nine feet or ten feet in width, the embankments were in places two feet above the surrounding ground, and the cuttings three feet deep. The road can be traced from the south-western corner of the mountain, with

K atherine Routledge.

one or two gaps, nearly to the foot of Rano Kao, but the succession of statues continues only about half the distance. … There are on this road twenty-seven statues in all, covering a distance of some four miles, but fourteen of them, including two groups of three, are in the first mile....

It was comparatively simple to trace two other roads from Raraku.... When the whole number of the statues on the roads were in imagination re-erected, it was found that they had all originally stood with their backs to the hill. Rano Raraku was, therefore, approached by at least three magnificent avenues, on each of which the pilgrim was greeted at intervals by a stone giant guarding the way to the sacred mountain....

Katherine Routledge
The Mystery of Easter Island
1919

The Archaeologists' Challenge

As an antidote to fanciful interpretations, scientists offer the results of their work. Who will succeed in solving the final mysteries of Easter Island?

A *moai* at Rano Raraku.

Collecting Oral Traditions

In countries where the main concern is to please the visitor, the degree of authenticity of the oral traditions depends on the quality of the informant and the date of the recording: Unfortunately the Easter Island Maori—that is, the individuals with the greatest knowledge of the subject —mostly disappeared in the raid of 1862 [by Peruvian slave hunters], before the first ethnographic investigations.

The first narratives were collected by Father Hippolyte Roussel, around 1870. After 1877 the Tahitian ancestry of Alexander Salmon, who settled on Easter Island as representative of the Brander firm, enabled him to maintain franker and no doubt closer relations with the 155 surviving islanders than the missionaries had been able to establish: Many traditional narratives were collected at this time thanks to his mediation. This is how the American William Thomson, despite the brevity of his stay in 1886 (from 18 to 30 December) was able to gather a large amount of documentation. Katherine Routledge, a wealthy Englishwoman, spent seventeen months on the island between 1914 and 1915. She produced a detailed study of the statues and obtained narratives from the last living representatives of the traditional culture; they were perhaps twenty years of age at the time of conversion. Unfortunately, most of her notes have been lost. Between 1934 and 1935, the expedition of Alfred Métraux and Henri Lavachery interviewed these individuals' children and grandchildren, who had never lived with the ancient gods.

Michel Orliac

New Evidence in Islanders' DNA

Where did the first Easter Islanders come from? Most anthropologists consider Polynesians, coming from the west, to be the most likely colonists.... But there has always been a flicker of doubt, a claim of South American ancestry fueled by controversial oral histories, claims of physical resemblances, and the trans-Pacific voyages of Thor Heyerdahl, who showed that sailing rafts like his famous *Kon-Tiki* could have made the trip from South America. Bones can also tell tales of prehistory, however, and, according to biochemist Erika Hagelberg, bones of ancient Easter Islanders contain genetic material that points unequivocally to Polynesian ancestry....

Mitochondrial DNA sequences she extracted from Easter Island skeletons proved identical to mtDNA sequences from living Polynesians and ancient Polynesian skeletons. Hagelberg used PCR [Polymerase Chain Reaction] to amplify mtDNA from 12 bone samples from Easter Island archaeological sites.... She then compared the sequences to sequences from bones exhumed elsewhere in Polynesia and from current Polynesians. One mtDNA sequence in particular is a signature of Polynesian ancestry. It has three single base-pair substitutions plus a nine base-pair deletion that have not been found in the mtDNA of any other ethnic group—and it turned up in the Easter Island bones. Conversely, sequences indicating Peruvian or Chilean ancestry were absent.... Hagelberg thinks the data put the notion of a South American connection to rest.

Joshua Fischman
Science, 262, 29 October 1993

The "Long Ears" and the "Short Ears"

Thor Heyerdahl has sought links with South America in the famous legend of the "long ears" (Hanau Eepe) and the "short ears" (Hanau Momoko), seeing the former as the descendants of the first (Amerindian) colonizers, and the latter as the more recent Polynesian arrivals. Hence he sees the "long ears" as having their earlobes elongated and perforated for disc-ornaments, a practice still current when the Europeans first arrived (though Mrs. Routledge was informed that the term "long ears" conveyed to the natives not the custom of distending the ears but having them long by nature). According to Heyerdahl's selected story, the "short ears" massacred all but one "long ear" (who subsequently had descendants) in the 17th century at the "battle of the Poike ditch."

Yet Sebastian Englert emphatically denied that these Polynesian terms referred to ears: having studied the older form of the islanders' language in more detail than anyone else, he stressed that the terms meant "broad/strong/corpulent people" and "slender people" respectively. In view of the widespread notion in Polynesia associating physical size and corpulency with leadership and *mana* (spiritual power), this would suggest that the Hanau Eepe were the upper class, and the Hanau Momoko the lower. Once again, the evidence for supposed links with the New World evaporates—and in any case…elongated ears and disc ornaments are well attested in the Marquesas Islands, and are therefore not exclusively a New World phenomenon.

Furthermore, Englert believed that the Hanau Eepe were latecomers who designed the platforms, and that the Hanau Momoko created the statues; while Thomas Barthel, after exhaustive study of the island's oral traditions, has decided that Hotu Matua arrived from Polynesia long after an initial colonization from the same direction—he was chief of the Hanau Momoko, but brought some Hanau Eepe prisoners with him as a labour force to work on the land. They were settled on Poike, away from the Momoko lands. Although the terms mean "slender" and "stocky" respectively, the tales concerning the two groups contain no indication of racial or cultural differences. It is far more likely that the relationship between them was one of victors and vanquished, or of lofty versus lowly status, although this clashes with

Entrance to an Easter Island cave.

the normal Polynesian association of stockiness with *mana* and the upper class.

Any attempt to fit the traditions to the archaeology is admirable, but... they are factually unreliable: at least six different genealogies have been recorded, for example, containing different names and numbers of kings, and these were gleaned from a few surviving natives from the late 19th century onwards, by then a decimated, demoralized and culturally impoverished population which had lost most of the collective cultural-historical memory.... The most probable hypothesis is still that of a single, early colonization from Polynesia, led by a chief, a culture hero who has been given the name Hotu Matua (i.e., Great Parent). The island's archaeological record is certainly one of continuous artifactual and architectural development, with no trace of a sudden influx of new cultural influences from outside.

Paul Bahn and John Flenley
Easter Island, Earth Island, 1992

Easter Island Rock Art

The rock art of Easter Island is an integral part of the total artistic output of the culture.... Animal imagery played a vital role in the ancient society. The important symbology that incorporates majestic seabirds throughout Polynesia is well described, as is that of fish and other sea forms.... It seems significant that, in all those instances where we were able to record legends associated with sea creature petroglyphs, the highlight of the stories was a magical ability to fly or swim away. These petroglyphs and their accompanying lore appear to be expressions of intense feelings of isolation and the desire to leave this lonely, confining island.... Not only does the petroglyphic

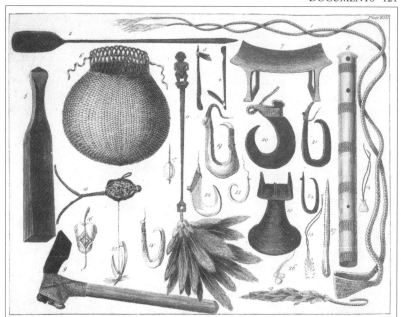

An 18th-century engraving showing various instruments and tools from Tahiti and neighboring islands.

inventory of Easter Island show amazing variety in design motifs, but the numbers, size, quality, and complexity of petroglyphs also vary considerably from one section of the island to another. Thus we may suggest a relation between design and social structure or function. Ritual or status-oriented carvings were meant to support and glorify the *ariki mau* or other priestly (or powerful) groups. Some of the finest rock art panels contrast with others that seemingly are casually made and poorly designed.... The image of the birdman appears in the rock art around AD 1550, a time of great stress and upheaval in the society.... This religion, perhaps fostered by a powerful priesthood, was an attempt to rejuvenate a dying society.... Orongo is ideally suited as the center for ceremonies concerning the new social order. It replaced the many locations around the island which were devoted to ancestor worship, and it likely had ceremonial importance and *mana* from the earliest settlement time.... The astonishing technical skill and artistic ability reflected in the rock art of Easter Island is found nowhere else in Polynesia.... For a small isolated population restricted to stone tools, the petroglyphs are extraordinary in their scope and quantity.

Georgia Lee
The Rock Art of Easter Island, 1992

Tools of Basalt and Obsidian

On Easter Island the tools were mostly made of stone; bone was used to make fishhooks and needles for sewing *tapa*; the sharp teeth of sharks were also much valued. The working of wood, focused entirely on small sculptures, was very limited in comparison with other Polynesian archipelagos; it required the use of small adzes, or *toki* in their language, of chisels (*kau toki* or *tingi*) and awls.... Conversely, the working of stone developed remarkably, whether in carving statues or in the making of facing slabs for the *ahu*, some of them located several miles from the quarry....

Crude picks, made in situ in the lapilli of the tuffs, exist in the hundreds in the statue quarries of Rano Raraku. The adzes were cut from a rock extracted from quarries at La Pérouse Bay, and the chisels from that of Mount Otu. Obsidian or volcanic glass, valued all over the world for its beauty and sharp edges, exists on Easter Island in abundance. It came primarily from Mount Orito, but there were other sources...of inferior quality. It was extracted in great flakes from tabular outcrops; the best-known finished products carved from this material are the *mataa*, tanged points with a wide variety of shapes that were used to arm spears; a great number of barely worked flakes were used in woodcarving.

Enigmatic Stone Towers: The *Tupa*

Along the shore and in the island's interior there are about thirty stone structures called *tupa*, whose function remains uncertain. They are edifices in the form of towers, oval or circular in plan, with a flat roof; a chamber about six to thirteen feet wide and ten feet high is fitted out inside; the access is through a low, narrow rectangular passage; these structures do not appear to have been dwellings, and have been interpreted in many different ways; some scholars think they were used by priests for observing the movement of heavenly bodies; these specialists could thus predict when turtles and migratory birds would arrive at the island, or determine the best time for planting.

A *tupa* at Vaihu.

The Orongo Houses

The village was inhabited from July to September for the birdman festivals. The oval or elliptical houses were arranged in two parallel rows; they measured from eight to thirty-three feet. They were made of a corbeling of rock slabs that constituted the roof of these structures, which was also covered with earth. The semiburied houses of Orongo had a low, narrow doorway, its lintel often decorated with engraved motifs; inside, opposite the door, upright stones were decorated with paintings of birdmen and dance-paddles and with depictions of the god Make Make. In front of each house there were earth-ovens for cooking food.

Catherine and Michel Orliac

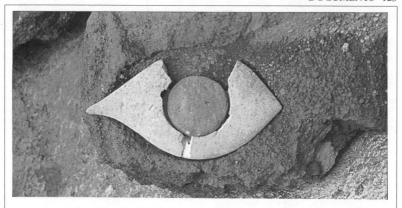

The Eyes of the Statues

The restoration in 1978 of the *ahu* Nau Nau, on the site of Anakena, brought an answer to one subject of controversy: the intriguing "gaze" of the statues. The sand that had accumulated through the years protected the *ahu* so well that it was easy to think that the statues had been toppled only yesterday. Something curious was found: about thirty pieces of coral, most of them as big as a fist, scattered near the broken statues.

The coral had been carved and polished. Fitting four pieces together produced an object with an unknown, oblong shape, 35 cm long. Sergio Rapu discovered that he had a *moai's* eye in his hands—or more precisely the eyeball, for a cavity was set in it for the iris, a disc of red volcanic tuff, slotted into a groove at the back of the eyeball, in its upper part. The eye fits the socket carved into the statue, and simply rests on a groove in the lower part, tilted so that it cannot fall: in this way the *moai* "looks at the stars."

One can say that all the *moai* on *ahu* had these eyes, albeit with small variations. For example, irises made of obsidian have been found during the restoration of *ahu* Tautira. One can see here an analogy with the wooden statuettes, whose eyes were made of shark vertebrae encrusted with an obsidian iris.

Now, let us go back in time. In 1886 the American [William] Thomson had thought of statues whose eyes had disappeared; [Henri] Lavachery had the same idea in 1935. During the 1960 restoration of *ahu* Akivi, [William] Mulloy had come very close to the discovery; he too had found fragments of coral and an almost intact eyeball, which he took to be a ceremonial bowl.

Coral does not exist naturally on Easter Island, and is brought to the coasts by the sea. In the 1930s a collection of coral was assembled to make whitewash, mainly in the western part of the island. It is probable that eyes disappeared then; the sands of Anakena have given them back.

Jacques Vignes
Les Mystères Résolus de l'Île de Pâques
(The Solved Mysteries of Easter Island)
1993

Enigmas and Foolishness

The mysteries surrounding the island have given rise not only to highly scientific theories but also to the most fanciful interpretations.

Colossal statues of the *ahu* Vaihu.

How the Stone Giants Were Moved

One of the great problems that dominate Easter Island archaeologically is the question of how the statues were moved to the *ahu*, some of which are miles from the quarry....

Many explanations have been given, some crazy and others unconvincing.

Some writers have suggested that a layer of sweet potatoes and yams was put under the statues—what a prodigious mess, stretching over miles and miles! Others have said that wooden rollers were used. But where would the unfortunate islanders have found the necessary timber? One has but to think of the stunted shoots of toromiro, all twisted by the wind, whose utmost girth is that of a man's thigh. Others have spoken of sledges.

To be sure, rope did exist, and we know its nature; it was tolerably strong, but even so one cannot possibly believe in these conjectures. There is another fact, even more surprising: the statues do not bear the least sign of a bump or a scratch; and when one considers the relative softness of this volcanic tufa it is clear that if the statues had been dragged on wooden rollers for miles they would bear the marks of it.

Reason naturally looks for logically satisfying evidence; but the most surprising thing is the unhesitating reply of all the natives—the statues were moved by *mana*. True or false, it is nevertheless very curious that the answer should always be the same. Our informants were categoric: only two men possessed *mana*. The people had to work hard to carve the *moai*, but when they were finished the king provided the *mana* to move them. These things are lost, they told us; there is no *mana* left.

It is a mistake to smile at this kind of talk, for if there is no valid logical explanation, why reject a hypothesis that may turn out to be true? What if certain men at a certain period were able to make use of electro-magnetic or anti-gravitational forces? It is an extraordinary concept, but not more so than that of squashed yams. And on the sheer side of the volcano there is something wonderfully strange. Here statues were brought down over the top of dozens of others, without leaving any marks. Yet the movement of ten or twenty tons is by no means child's play.

One should not indulge in the kind of reasoning that says "If such exceptional things existed then the civilization must have been exceptional too; and we know that it had only reached the neolithic age." This is not really very sound, for in Africa, for example, we know of many striking abnormalities that nevertheless run constantly parallel to a society of the kind called stationary or regressive.

I find it hard to believe in what I have just set forth, but I cannot reject what may be a probability. After all, scarcely twenty years ago orthodox archaeology held that the earliest date for the appearance of man could not go back beyond 100,000 BC; and since we are now very far from that reasonable…dating, I am uneasy about all so-called possibilities. I am all the more uneasy because the natives say that everything died on Easter Island when *mana* left it, while at the same time I see the amazing evidence of a quite extraordinary past. It may be that para-psychology will find a sympathetic vibration in this island with its perturbed, confusing magnetism.

At this point I recall something else a native told me. He said that the statues moved standing upright, making half turns on their round bases. This really does give the impression of an electro-magnetic mechanism at work in a restricted field.

As for the setting up of the statues on the *ahu*…when one is confronted with a statue that measures seventy-two feet (the height of a seven-storey house) and that lies almost completed upon the Rano-Raraku cliff, then logic is silenced. Think of the head and neck twenty-three feet long and ten broad, the nose twelve feet long and the body forty-three. Fifty tons! Even now there are few cranes in the world that can lift such a mass. Yet there the statue is, framed in its two access-trenches, already three-quarters finished. And it was never made to stay there like a vast relief in the rock. It was made to be raised. The head sculptor knew what he was doing: he certainly intended to bring this giant to life.

In order to take away the famous statue called "the Wave-breaker," which is only seven and a half feet high, more than five hundred men were needed, and they had winches and all the necessary material. With all her equipment and men, the French corvette *La Flore* could only manage to bring back one head, and much battered at that, now in the Musée de l'Homme. Easter Island had no trees, and there was little likelihood of producing a continual supply of fresh rope: with its five thousand inhabitants or thereabouts it was not Egypt, nor yet Tiahuanaco, where some archaeologists postulate an army of slaves.

So it is better either to say that the mystery remains unsolved or that the answer is on a completely different plane—that it is fantastic.

Francis Mazière
Mysteries of Easter Island, 1969

Even More Foolish Theories

The first European seafarers who landed on Easter Island at the beginning of the 18th century could scarcely believe their eyes. On this little plot of earth, 2250 miles from the coast of Chile, they saw hundreds of colossal statues, which lay scattered about all over the island. Whole mountain massifs had been transformed, steel-hard volcanic rock had been cut through like butter and 10,000 tons of massive rocks lay in places where they could not have been dressed. Hundreds of gigantic statues, some of which are between 33 and 66 ft. high and weigh as much as 50 tons, still stare challengingly at the visitor today—like robots which seem to be waiting solely to be set in motion again.…

Easter Island lies far away from any continent or civilization. The islanders are more familiar with moon and stars than any other country. No trees grow on the island, which is a tiny speck of volcanic stone. The usual explanation, that the stone giants were moved to their present sites on wooden rollers, is not feasible in this case, either. In addition the island can scarcely have provided food for more than 2000 inhabitants. (A few hundred natives live on Easter Island today.) A shipping trade, which brought food and clothing to the island for the stonemasons, is hardly credible in antiquity. Then who cut the statues out of the rock, who carved them and transported them to their sites? How were they moved across country for miles without rollers? How were they dressed, polished and erected? How were the hats, the stone for which

Giant statues lying in the quarry of Rano Raraku.

came from a different quarry from that of the statues, put in place?… Who did do the work?… Unfortunately the first missionaries…burnt the tablets with hieroglyphic characters, they prohibited the ancient cults of the gods and did away with every kind of tradition. Yet…they could not prevent the natives from calling their island the "Land of the bird men," as they still do today. An orally transmitted legend tells us that flying men landed and lit fires in ancient times. The legend is confirmed by sculptures of flying creatures with big staring eyes.

Connexions between Easter Island and Tiahuanaco automatically force themselves upon us. There as here, we find stone giants belonging to the same style. The haughty faces with their stoic expressions suit the statues—here as there. When Francisco Pizarro questioned the Incas about Tiahuanaco in 1532, they told him that no man had ever seen the city save in ruins, for Tiahuanaco had been built in the night of mankind. Traditions call Easter Island the "navel of the world." It is more than 3125 miles from Tiahuanaco to Easter Island. How can one culture possibly have inspired the other?…

The unknown space travellers who visited our planet many thousands of years ago can hardly have been less farsighted than we think we are today. They were convinced that one day man would make the move out into the universe on his own initiative and using his own skills. It is a well-known historical fact that the intelligences of our planet have constantly sought for kindred spirits, for life, for corresponding intelligences in the cosmos.

Erich Von Däniken
Chariots of the Gods?
1969

Easter Island seen from the sea.

The Tree of the Easter Islanders

The toromiro (Sophora toromiro Skottsb.), *which used to grow in great numbers on Easter Island, is a small leguminous tree with yellow flowers. Its beautiful and resistant wood was used for making, among other things, the famous* moai kava kava.

Björn Aldén (above right) carrying a toromiro seedling (branch of tree opposite).

Around 1956, a few years before the last toromiro disappeared from Easter Island, Thor Heyerdahl led an archaeological expedition to the island. Professor Olof Selling, a Swedish palynologist [a scientist specializing in pollen and spores], had asked him to collect a few peat samples from Rano Kao, and it was while he was carrying out this duty that he heard of the last toromiro specimens, which were growing almost at the base of the crater. He went there, but could find only a single tree that seemed to be in a very bad condition. He removed one of the living branches bearing seed-filled pods, and sent it to Professor Selling, who, two years later, realized the importance of these pods and had them taken to the Botanical Garden of Göteborg. The seeds germinated in the spring of 1959, and then the seedlings produced mature plants. Today two of them are still alive in our greenhouses.

In 1980 a decision was taken to try to reintroduce the toromiro on Easter Island, and three rooted cuttings were sent there through the French photographer Christian Zuber.

The following year, one of our Göteborg toromiros flowered for the first time, and two years later seeds from this tree were sent to the island.

Unfortunately, none of these attempts was crowned with success: A root nematode appeared on the island and killed all the seedlings. However, other seedlings and cuttings were produced at Göteborg and, at the same time, a project of "micropropagation" was set up in collaboration with the Swedish University of Agriculture.

In autumn 1987 I accepted Thor Heyerdahl's invitation to accompany him to Easter Island to make another, much publicized, attempt. Two

vigorous seedlings, about two feet tall, were given special treatment and, on 12 February 1988, were taken by me on a plane to Easter Island, where I was warmly welcomed.

The seedlings were finally planted on 17 February 1988 in a private garden at Hanga Roa using fresh earth, free from nematodes, brought from the shores of Rano Aroi. We very carefully set the first seedling in place under the supervision of Mr. Gerardo Velasco, the island's foremost agronomist. I shall never forget that moment; I had the feeling that finally, this time, the toromiro was going to survive.

Unfortunately, my feelings were unjustified. Even now (1995) there are no well-established toromiros on Easter Island. Although the original material of *S. toromiro* is to be found only in Göteborg—all known toromiros seem to originate from one single tree—there are a few gardens where the true species has been cultivated for a long period.

Propagation has produced hundreds of small plants, which can be distributed to other gardens or can be replanted on Easter Island.

Cooperation with other botanical gardens has been—and remains—of central importance. One project, started in 1993, successfully established the toromiro for the first time in open ground in Europe—in the Jardin Botanique Exotique at Menton in southern France.

Another important step was taken in 1994 when, on the initiative of four European botanic gardens, including the Royal Botanic Gardens, Kew, a special Toromiro Management Group was created. It will cooperate in a larger reintroduction project and will look into the existence of other true toromiros in cultivation, with the aim of enlarging the dangerously low gene pool of *S. toromiro*.

Björn Aldén
Botanical Garden of Göteborg, Sweden

The Importance of Adornment

Ethnologist Alfred Métraux was the source of most of our knowledge about the Easter Islanders' traditional life. He gathered his information during an expedition—from 27 July 1934 to 2 January 1935 —that he led with the Belgian archaeologist Henri Lavachery.

Dress and Personal Adornment

The men used to wear nothing but a wide belt of beaten bark, one end of which was passed between the legs and hung down over the abdomen. To keep off the cold, or merely for the sake of elegance, they cast about their shoulders a rectangular cape stained with turmeric. The women wore a similar belt and sometimes a short skirt. They also liked to wrap themselves in a bark cloak.

The hair of both men and women fell loose to their shoulders or was knotted in a tuft on top of their heads. In a love song a woman's top-knot is compared to the fin of a fish:

Young girl, you are dying of love.
You are a crab living under
    Akurenga mausoleum,
You are a fish with a top-knot.
You make for the shore,
Little fish, O my friend!
Down there is seaweed
That is good to feed you.

There was little scope for personal vanity in clothes or hair-style; this found expression in the tattooing that made some men's bodies real works of art. Loti and other travellers made drawings of the patterns which the Easter Islanders tattooed on their persons. In the variety and intricacy of its motifs and their unexpected and ingenious arrangement, Easter Island tattooing falls little short artistically of that produced by the Marquesans and Maoris—the peoples who have carried this art to the highest degree of perfection. Easter tattooing is characterized by the important role of areas of geometric form spread over the face and other parts of the body.

Another of its peculiarities is the frequent use of naturalistic motifs, representing birds, plants and implements. The native whose tattooing was copied down by Stolpe bore on his arm a picture of the Orongo statue being carried off by the sailors of the *Topaze*. Close perpendicular lines tattooed on the thighs and lower legs gave many natives the appearance of wearing stockings or breeches.

These works of art were produced by experts who supplied their services to those who could afford to pay for them. An individual's rank and affluence were often indicated by the extent and beauty of the patterns covering his body. The operation was slow and carried out at intervals of several years. For tattooing to be perfect when the subject reached adulthood, it had to be started early—generally at the age of eight. The tattooist's instrument was a little bone rake, which he tapped with a mallet to drive it into the epidermis. The pigment was charcoal made from *ti* stems mixed with *poporo* (*Solanum nigrum*) juice. These sessions were painful, and some children—such as Viriamo, whose tattooing remained unfinished—were unable to endure them. The chief source of our knowledge of Easter Island tattooing are two *tapa* images now in the Peabody Museum, Harvard. They are covered with painted drawings which reproduce with great care the most common tattoo patterns.…

The effects of tattooing were enhanced by painting the body with red, white and grey earths, and especially with powder extracted from the turmeric. The popularity of this latter root was due not only to the orange pigment obtained from it, but also to its perfume. The scent it emits is regarded by Polynesians as particularly delectable, but Europeans are insensible to it. In olden times the perfumed emanations of the Rano-raraku turmeric attracted two spirit-women who were living *i te hiva*, in a foreign land, and who flew to Easter Island to see these marvellous plants. The myth adds that it was they who taught the islanders' ancestors the delicate method by which the famous *pua* powder is prepared.

Red and black were the favourite colours of the men. They smeared their faces with alternate stripes in these two colours. Men blackened from head to foot made a tremendous impression on the first Europeans who saw them, as may be gathered from Beechey's account.

Easter Island might have been called the "Land of the Long-Eared Men." The natives described by the first voyagers had the lobes of their ears widely perforated to make room for the insertion of a heavy ornament made of shark's vertebrae or wood. This practice was abandoned at the period when native culture vanished, and the last old people with deformed ears died at the beginning of the present century.

The finest ornaments were cock-feather diadems of various shapes and colours, and especially reed helmets covered with feather mosaic. The women wore strange wicker-work hats, wide and rounded at the sides and with turned-up points at the back and front.

The old Easter Islanders had a passion for headgear and to satisfy it they risked the retaliation of the Europeans whose caps they stole. Their taste sometimes had comical results. Eyraud relates in one of his letters that there was no object of which they would not make a hat. A calabash, half a melon, the carcass of a bird—anything would do. One native even proudly set on his head two buckets one inside the other. The most amusing case, however, was that of a man who, having found a shoe, shod his head. These sartorial extravagances came to an end after the period of assimilation.

The portrait of an old Easter Islander in gala dress is incomplete until the wooden ornaments with which he decorated himself have been enumer-

ated. If he was rich and noble he hung on his chest a large crescent (*rei-miro*), whose carved horns represented bearded men or cocks. Others attached to their shoulders *tahonga*, a sort of wooden "heart," which some writers have interpreted as stylized coconuts. These objects for indicating wealth have never been seen displayed by a modern traveller. We know them from the accounts of the living natives and the specimens that have found their way into our museums.

Tepano took delight in enumerating these wooden treasures. They are the subject of the same legends as are current regarding the tablets. During our stay, more than one islander, inspired by a dream, set out to look for caves full of *rei-miro*, *tahonga* and statuettes, for dreams of wealth are

still nourished by the memory of these wooden adornments....

The Origin of Tattooing: An Easter Island Myth

The Lizard Woman and the Gannet Woman came from their house at Hakarava and went to the bay of Hanga-takaure. The Lizard Woman asked: "What is the name of this *ahu*?" "It is Hanga-takaure, the name of this land," answered the Gannet Woman. "What is Hanga-takaure to myself and to two beautiful women, the Lizard Woman and the Gannet Woman?" They continued along the south coast and at each settlement the elder sister, the Lizard Woman, asked her younger sister, the Gannet Woman, for the name of the place. When she had been told she always replied; "What is this place to myself, and to two beautiful girls, the Lizard Woman and the Gannet Woman?" The two sisters dived into the water and swam to Motu-nui. They stayed there and slept with the young men Heru and Patu. They became pregnant, gave birth to children, and reared them until they were grown. These two women were tattooed on the thighs, the cheek bones, the throat, the lips, the forearms, the jaws, and marked with circles on the buttocks.

The husbands went to Poike on the main island and slept with two other women who became pregnant and gave birth to children. The husbands returned to Motu-nui.

The children of the Lizard Woman and the Gannet Woman had been tattooed on the legs and jaws. They went to the main island and arrived at Orongo. The older one jumped on a stone of unusual size and shouted: "Look at me, brother, as the red new

moon." The younger one sprang on a small stone and said: "Look at me like the round moon." They went to Vinapu, to Maherenga, and to Papa-tangaroa-hiro in search of surf-riding. Finally at Otuu they saw men, women, and children watching the surf-riders and the breaking waves. The young men asked the people for surf boards and went out to where the waves were breaking. A big wave reached its peak, then came a flat wave; the young men were carried on the waves and landed on shore. The people shouted: "The surf-riders have landed!" The young men returned the boards to their owners. They went away and bathed in fresh water, then sat by a rock.

Two boys went to a well and drew water. The young men, sons of the Lizard Woman and the Gannet Woman, made a spell and broke their calabashes. "Why have you broken our calabashes?" asked the boys. "We don't know. Who are you?" asked the young men. "We are the sons of Heru and Patu," replied the young men. "How could you be sons of Heru and Patu, you are crabs, crayfish and octopuses." The two men told their father what the young men had said, and the father said: "Go and fetch these young men." The two ugly men went to

get the young men and together they went to the house of the father. The two young men went into another house where there were two girls. They stayed there and were fed with chicken, sweet potatoes, and fish by the father. They seized the girls to sleep with them but the girls did not want that. In the morning the girls saw how beautiful the two young men were and fell in love with them. They seized them and pulled them about, but the young men did not want them. So the young men left and went toward Hanga-nui. The girls followed them to Orohie, to Maio, to Papa-haka-heruru. The young men arrived at Vaikaranga and entered a long feast-house for boys and girls. Inside were two ugly girls called Angu, who were jealous when they saw the good-looking girls called Hangu-arai, and decided to deceive them. All the girls went to the shore to bathe. The ugly Angu said: "Let us go to the rocks and jump." The Hangu-arai girls replied: "You jump first and we will jump after you." One of the Angu jumped. "May she sleep on the rock," said the Hangu-arai. The other ugly Angu said: "She is dead." "No she is just asleep," said the Hangu-arai, "you jump and be finished." The other Angu jumped and died. The Hangu-arai then returned to their husbands, Heru and Patu.

The two mothers stayed on the island. One day the elder went to a heap of rock called Rangi-manu and shouted to the sea: "You Vivivivi and Vaovao come and tear me to pieces." They came and lacerated her and she died. Then the younger sister did the same thing.

Alfred Métraux
Easter Island
Translated by Michael Bullock
1957

Coping with Change on Easter Island

Shortly before noon each Wednesday, an aging LAN-Chile Boeing 707 thundered down the runway at Santiago's Arturo Merino Benítez Airport. As the plane climbed, the passengers settled back for a five-hour flight across the spectacular cloudscapes of the South Pacific. The 707's destination was Chile's Easter Island...2350 miles west of the mainland.

For Easter Island's 2060 residents, the plane's weekly arrival merits a ritual celebration. The terminal is thronged with Pascuences, or natives of Polynesian stock, and "Conties," as the minority Chilean mainlanders are known. Guides eagerly welcome a handful of tourists with garlands of white hibiscus. Relatives greet returning residents in singsong Rapa Nui, the island language that is still taught in school. As airport workers unload cargo, including mail and videocassettes containing mainland television programs, the talk turns swiftly to Topic A on Easter Island: the trucks and earth-moving equipment that are extending the 9500-foot airstrip to permit an emergency landing by NASA's troubled space shuttle—if and when it ever goes into polar orbit.

The eight-month construction job, costing $7 million and funded by the U.S., should not directly disturb the 600-odd *moai* stone statues, some dating from as early as AD 1100. Nonetheless the project remains controversial. When the regime of Augusto Pinochet gave the U.S. the

P eople of Easter Island.

go-ahead last year [in 1985], the local people had not been consulted. Navy Captain Francisco Santana, the ranking military officer on the island, argues that the longer airstrip "will be a big advantage, producing a shower of money." Yet Alberto Hotus, fifty-six, president of the council of elders, an informal committee representing thirty-six family groups, complains that while the improved airfield may benefit Conti contractors and, ultimately, airlines, "it is difficult to see what we get out of it."

Hotus charges that laborers brought from the mainland earn four times the wages of locals. Further, archaeologists fear that construction workers searching for landfill will damage some of the thousands of archaeological structures that still lie buried. Says a longtime foreign resident: "Every hillock and practically every rock and puddle has a name. When you move earth, you are destroying a name."

The concern reflects the islanders' pride in the impassive stone statues that stand like sentinels on the sloping hills. Easter Island has few natural endowments. "We live from the land, the fish and the tourists," explains Juan Chaves, vice president of the elders. "But if we lose the archaeological sites, twenty or thirty years from now, what do we have left?"

When Heyerdahl, now seventy-one, arrived on Easter Island in 1955 to buttress his controversial theory that Polynesia was settled by emigrants from ancient Peru, he recalls that "poverty was everywhere. The people were in rags." "There was no money, only barter, and clothes, shoes and rice came from the company store," adds Pedro Avaca Pakanio, sixty-five, leader of thirty tuna fishermen in

Hanga Roa, the island's sole town....

In those days, the island was administered by the Chilean navy, which did little except enforce naval law and announce the time by ship's bell. The neglect ended in 1966, when the islanders were granted Chilean citizenship, an airstrip was built, and weekly flights brought regular contact with the outside world....

Development by outsiders is discouraged by a 1979 law that prohibits anyone except native Easter Islanders or the Chilean government from owning land: indeed, 90% of the island either belongs to a government development corporation or is part of a national park. More than half of the seven hundred local workers are employed by the state, which budgets about $6 million annually for the island's upkeep. Others must find jobs as fishermen, as guides for the two thousand tourists who come to view the statues each year or as subsistence farmers.

Gavin Scott
Time, 15 September 1986

A house at Orongo where the religious ceremonies of the birdman festival took place.

Chronology

The first archaeological chronology of Easter Island was established by William Mulloy, based on the studies carried out by the Norwegian expedition and published in 1961. Three periods were distinguished: the early period (400–1100), the middle period (1100–1680), and the late period (1680–1868). Recent work by Edwin Ferdon (1961), William S. Ayres (1975–81), Christopher M. Stevenson (1984), and JoAnne Van Tilburg (1986) has expanded this tripartite division.

EARLY PERIOD 400–1100?	*Phase of settling down and development* Statues must have been erected before 700. According to Arne Skjölsvold, these statues are smaller than those of the next phase; naturalistic in style, they preceded the standardized sculptures of Rano Raraku. According to Van Tilburg, there are two morphological types, probably even three. At the end of this phase, there is an *ahu* on the site of Orongo. Little is known about the details of daily life in this period.
MIDDLE PERIOD 1100–1680 (OR 1000–1500)	*Phase of expansion, or* Ahu Moai *phase* Architecture reached its peak at the start of this period. The *ahu* diversify and increase in size; the rear wall of some displays a facing of well-fitted slabs; the *moai* erected on the *ahu* platform become stereotyped and grow bigger and bigger, probably a sign of competition between the lineages and a mark of the preeminence of chiefs over priests. The extraction of the statues in the slopes of Rano Raraku occurs between 1000 and 1500. The headdresses of the *moai*, made of red tuff, are later than 1500 and last until the end of the expansion phase. The organization of the villages and the form of the houses are known. Based on archaeological evidence, the population is estimated at nine thousand around the year 1600. At Orongo, around 1400, stone houses are constructed, oval in shape; but the oldest dwellings with thick drystone walls would be built on this site only after 1540. The occupation of caves has been dated to not earlier than the end of the expansion phase.
LATE PERIOD 1680 (OR 1500)–1722	*Decadent phase, or* Huri Moai *phase* No *ahu moai* is built during this phase; most of those that existed are destroyed or abandoned. Semipyramidal *ahu* are constructed and used as tombs. Tools are similar to those of the preceding periods, but the *mataa*, obsidian spear points, seem to multiply around 1700. The opposition between the east and west territorial entities becomes flagrant, and the birdman cult develops. This phase ends with Roggeveen's arrival.
PROTOHISTORIC PERIOD 1722–1868	The *ahu* continue to be used as tombs; in many cases bones, grouped in bundles, are simply placed there under the stones. Contact with Europeans brings important changes. The population is estimated at 9600 around the year 1800, and 8200 around 1850. The end of this phase coincides with the conversion to Christianity.
HISTORICAL PERIOD SINCE 1868	At the start of this phase, the population is concentrated in the southwest part of the island. In 1877 there are no more than 111 individuals following the abductions by Peruvian slave hunters, the epidemics, and the departure of islanders for Tahiti. The *ahu*, sometimes still used as tombs at the beginning of the 20th century, lose their religious function completely.

Michel Orliac

Further Reading

Bahn, Paul G., and John Flenley, *Easter Island, Earth Island*, Thames and Hudson, New York, 1992

Beechey, Frederick William, *Narrative of a Voyage to the Pacific and Beering's Strait…In the Years 1825–1828*, 2 vols., H. Colburn & R. Bentley, London, 1831

Behrens, Carl Friederich, *Another Narrative of Jacob Roggeveen's Visit*, 1908

Choris, Louis, *Voyage Pittoresque Autour du Monde*, Imprimérie de Firmin Didot, Paris, 1822

Cook, James, *A Voyage Towards the South Pole, and Round the World…In the Years 1772–1775*, Libraries Board of South Australia, Adelaide, Australia, repr. 1970

Dupetit-Thouars, Abel, *Voyage Autour du Monde sur la Frégate la Vénus, Pendant les Années 1836–1839*, Gide, Paris, 1840–64

Englert, Sebastian, *Island at the Center of the World: New Light on Easter Island*, trans. and ed. William Mulloy, Scribner, New York, 1970

Fischer, Steven R., ed., *Easter Island Studies: Contributions to the History of Rapanui in Memory of William T. Mulloy*, 1993

Forster, Johann Reinhold, *The Resolution Journal of Johann Reinhold Forster, 1772–1775*, ed. Michael E. Hoare, 4 vols., Clarendon Press, Oxford, England, 1982

González y Haedo, Felipe, *The Voyage of Captain Don Felipe González in the Ship of Line San Lorenzo …to Easter Island in 1770–1771*, Hakluyt Society, Cambridge, 1908

Heyerdahl, Thor, *The Art of Easter Island*, Doubleday, Garden City, New York, 1975

———, *Easter Island—The Mystery Solved*, Souvenir Press, London, 1989

Heyerdahl, Thor, and Edwin Nelson Ferdon, eds., *Reports of the Norwegian Archaeological Expedition to Easter Island and the East Pacific*, vol. 1: *The Archaeology of Easter Island*, 1961; vol. 2: *Miscellaneous Papers*, 1965

Kotzebue, Otto von, *A Voyage of Discovery into the South Seas and Beering's Straits… 1815–1818*, London, 1821

La Pérouse, Jean-François de Galaup, Comte de, *A Voyage Round the World in the Years 1785–1788*, 3 vols., 1798

Lee, Georgia, *The Rock Art of Easter Island: Symbols of Power, Prayers to the Gods*, Institute of Archaeology, University of California, Los Angeles, 1992

Lisianski, Urey, *Voyage Round the World 1803–1806 in the Ship Neva*, J. Boork and Longman Hurst, 1814

Loti, Pierre, *L'Ile de Pâques, Journal d'Un Aspirant de la Flore*, 1988

Machowski, Jacek, *Island of Secrets: The Discovery and Exploration of Easter Island*, trans. Maurice Michael, Hale, London, 1975

McCall, Grant, *Rapanui: Tradition and Survival on Easter Island*, 1994

Mellén Blanco, Francisco, *Manuscritos y Documentos Españoles para la Historia de la Isla de Pascua*, 1986

Métraux, Alfred, *Easter Island*, trans. Michael Bullock, Oxford University Press, New York, 1957

———, *Ethnology of Easter Island*, 1940

Picker, Fred, *Rapa Nui*, Paddington Press, New York, 1974

Roggeveen, Jacob, *The Journal of Jacob Roggeveen*, trans. and ed. Andrew Sharp, 1970

Routledge, Katherine, *The Mystery of Easter Island*, Sifton, Praed & Co., London, 1919

Sharan, Mahesh Kumar, Abhinav Publications, New Delhi, India, 1974

Thomson, William J., *Te Pito te Henua or Easter Island: U.S. National Museum Annual Report for the Year Ending 1889*, Government Printing Office, Washington, D.C., 1891

List of Illustrations

Index